ON THE UNITY OF CHRIST

ST CYRIL OF ALEXANDRIA
ON THE UNITY OF CHRIST

Translated and with an Introduction

by

JOHN ANTHONY MCGUCKIN

ST VLADIMIR'S SEMINARY PRESS
CRESTWOOD, NY 10707
1995

Library of Congress Cataloging-in-Publication Data

Cyril, Saint, Patriarch of Alexandria, ca. 370-444
    [Hoti heis ho Christos. English]
    On the unity of Christ / St. Cyril of Alexandria: translated and with an
introduction by John Anthony McGuckin.
       p.   cm.
    Includes bibliographical references and index.
    ISBN 0-88141-133-7
    1. Jesus Christ-Person and offices–Early works to 1800. I McGuckin,
John Anthony. II. Title
BR65.C953H6813   1995
232-dc20   95-18709
                                                        CIP

Translation © 1995
St Vladimir's Seminary Press

ISBN 0-88141-133-7

PRINTED IN THE UNITED STATES OF AMERICA

Contents

ABBREVIATIONS 6

PREFACE 7

INTRODUCTION 9

    The Life of St Cyril 9
    A Synopsis of St Cyril's Christological Doctrine 32

ON THE UNITY OF CHRIST 49

SELECT BIBLIOGRAPHY 135

    A. *Texts and Translations of St Cyril* 135
    B. *Select Bibliography of General Studies* 137
    C. *Select Bibliography of Cyrilline Studies* 138
    D. *Select Bibliography on Antiochene Christology* 141

INDEX 143

INDEX OF BIBLICAL REFERENCES 147

Abbreviations

ACO	*Acta Conciliorum Oecumenicorum* (E.Schwartz)
CHR	*Catholic Historical Review* (Washington)
CSCO	*Corpus Scriptorum Christianorum Orientalium*
DOP	*Dumbarton Oaks Papers*
Ep	Epistle
ET	English Translation
GOTR	*Greek Orthodox Theological Review* (Brookline)
ITQ	*Irish Theological Quarterly* (Maynooth)
JEH	*Journal of Ecclesiastical History* (Cambridge)
JTS	*Journal of Theological Studies* (Oxford) NS = New Series
PBR	*Patristic and Byzantine Review* (New York)
PG	*Cursus Completus Patrologiae Graecae* (J.P. Migne)
PL	*Cursus Completus Patrologiae Latinae* (J. P. Migne)
ROC	*Revue de L'Orient Chrétien* (Paris)
SC	*Sources Chrétiennes* (Paris)
Stud. Pat.	*Studia Patristica*
TU	*Texte und Untersuchungen* (Berlin)

PREFACE

It is one and the same Holy Spirit, which the Fathers at Nicaea had within them as they defined the faith, which was in the soul and voice of our most holy and venerable Father the Archbishop Cyril when he dictated this for the correction of the errors that the reverend Nestorius introduced to the church.

Bishop Hermogenes of Rhinocourouros
(Acclamation at the Council of Ephesus
after the reading of Cyril's writings against Nestorius)

INTRODUCTION

The Life of St Cyril

The city of Alexandria had long been the main port of supplies for imperial Rome, and from the beginnings of the Roman Empire, therefore, had grown in importance along with the capital. Its earlier glories as a world center of learning under the Ptolemies were not forgotten in its new role as provincial imperial capital, and it was always more a Greek city than a Roman one. By the time of the early Byzantine period, in the fourth century, its identity as a major political and cultural force had not abated. Provincial governors in Egypt were men of immense power whom emperors could not overlook. By the fifth century that role passed more and more to the ecclesiastical leaders of the city, as the Christian population took the ascendancy from the other two major civic groups, the large Jewish community, and the educated philosophic class who still made Alexandria a focus for a continuing pagan opposition to the Christian way of life.

In the time of Constantine the Great, the Christian bishop of Alexandria, St Athanasius, showed how much power and influence a determined Christian archon could wield in opposition to the state bureaucracy. The forces at his disposal included not only the large congregations of a very volatile populace, but specially organized guilds and, not far away from the city itself, large bodies of men living the new forms of ascetical life that came to be called monasticism. The successors of St Athanasius capitalized on the archiepiscopal role, and soon the Patriarchate of Alexandria was known throughout the Christian world as a leading force in the formulation of Christian doctrine and a

guiding hand in so many matters of canonical importance.
From the third century, the Christian theologians of Alexandria
were internationally famous and each in their own way developed a distinctive and coherent school of thought: thinkers such
as Pantaenus, Clement, Origen, Alexander, and Athanasius.
Cyril stands in a long line of illustrious predecessors, and he is
very conscious of continuing their work.

Before the rise of Constantinople to ecclesiastical eminence
in the late fourth century, the sees of Rome and Alexandria were
the undisputed leaders of Christian opinion, and Alexandria had
long regarded itself as the mentor of Eastern Christian life, a role
it was loath to relinquish to the new ascendant star on the shores
of the Bosphorus. Many of these wider political and canonical
factors caused great unrest in the internal and external relations of
the church from the fourth to the sixth centuries. St Gregory the
Theologian's complaints against the machinations of the Egyptian
hierarchs at the Council of Constantinople (381) and the condemnation of St John Chrysostom at the Synod of the Oak (403)
represent scenes in this long-running drama.

One of the most dominant ecclesiastical leaders of Alexandria was St Theophilus,[1] who was archbishop from 385-412.
He used the power base of his throne to put into effect new
imperial legislation suppressing pagan temples. In Alexandria
this caused city riots on a grand scale, but Theophilus pressed
into service bands of determined monks, and by this means
destroyed some of the city's most ancient pagan temples such
as the Serapeum, in 391, and turned others into Christian
churches. His occupancy of the throne marks the emergence of
Alexandria as a predominantly Christian city. Theophilus had
great ambitions for his city and his see. He maneuvred against
St John Chrysostom, to block the latter's reformist moves in
Constantinople, and by bringing about the downfall of the newly

1 Feast Day: Oct. 15th (Coptic); Oct. 17th (Syrian).

appointed archbishop he safeguarded the traditional sphere of influence of his own see, ranging as it did from Libya, to Palestine, and the Roman Province of Asia (modern Turkey).

This powerful hierarch summoned his sister's son to the city to advance his education and train him in the affairs of church governance. The young boy, Cyril, was born in 378 and came under his uncle's tutelage from his twelfth year onwards. He probably studied grammar and rhetoric in the city until approximately the year 397, and then followed a period of specifically Christian higher studies. His knowledge of the Bible was profound, and in his youth the school of Alexandria was at a high point under the great exegete Didymus the Blind (†398). This period of formal theological and scriptural study introduced him to the earlier tradition of the Church, and he always regarded himself as a continuer of that tradition. In fact, it was Cyril who largely started the Christian theological method of appealing to prior patristic writings to determine what the tradition was, citing their texts as evidence of "the mind of the saints." His knowledge of the earlier Alexandrian theologians (especially St Athanasius), the exegetical works of St Chrysostom, and the doctrinal works of St Gregory the Theologian is extensive, and is put to good use in his own writings.

In 403 Cyril was ordained lector of the church at Alexandria, a position that carried with it intellectual and administrative duties at the archbishop's court. Later that year he attended the Synod of the Oak in the company of his uncle Theophilus. When he became archbishop himself, he still regarded Chrysostom as having been justly condemned for canonical irregularities[2] and was only later persuaded to regard him as innocent, after the application of considerable pressure from Rome and the imperial court at Constantinople.

When Theophilus died in October 412, the Byzantine ad-

2 Cf. Cyril's Letter 76, PG 77:351-360.

ministration attempted to block Cyril's election, and supported the incumbent archdeacon Timothy. It is a testament to Cyril's large body of support within the local church that despite the backing his rival had from the local garrison, it was Cyril who was elected as Theophilus' successor, and consecrated on October 18, 412. The election was contested and both factions came to blows.[3] So it was that at 34 years of age Cyril's career as one of the leading hierarchs of the Byzantine world began in the turbulent environment of Alexandria.

The early years of Cyril's administration showed him as a reformer. He made moves against the continuing influence that pagan religion still had on the minds of the common people, but unlike his uncle he chose to meet the allurements of the Isis cult on a different, more subtle, battle ground. One example of this new strategy was his removal of the relics of the martyr saints Cyrus and John to Menouthis, where a great Temple of Isis still flourished, offering healing cures to devotees. Cyril installed the relics of the martyrs in the small church nearby and instituted Christian healing rites to prevent, as he said, Christians from being led astray. The Menouthis Temple was a healing center with its own staff of medical priests. Cyril's concern to ensure the Church met and bettered any benefit that paganism could supply was a major influence on Christian missionary strategy, and he staffed the new Christian shrine with monastics, providing a pattern that Christianity would continue for many centuries.[4]

Still other problems beset him in regard to the volatile political and religious factions that made Alexandria a difficult city to govern. Not least among them was the Church's continuing friction with Judaism. The Jewish community was

3 Cf. Socrates, *Church History* 7:7.

4 Cf. J. A. McGuckin, "The Influence of the Isis Cult on the Christology of St Cyril of Alexandria," Stud. Pat. 24. (1992), 191-99.

extensive and had a long and eminent history in Alexandria. It enjoyed an intellectual tradition that had produced no less than Philo, and the writers of much of the Old Testament Wisdom literature. This sizeable proportion of the city was in no mood to acquiesce in the political ascendancy of the Christians, despite much legislation emanating from the court of Theodosius II that progressively restricted their own civic rights.

On one occasion the ever-present tension between the Jewish and Christian communities erupted in a local incident where a church was burned and some leading Christians assassinated. In response Cyril led a delegation of the church to the Jewish quarter to demand justice. In this he was acting as the Christian archon, the ethnic and religious leader of the Christian population, and independently of the Byzantine City Governor Orestes. The latter disliked Cyril intensely and regarded his growing power with dismay as dangerously eclipsing his own. Cyril's delegation degenerated into popular riots and several synagogues were burned which supposedly were those of the anti-Christian agitators. The attack on the Jewish community was followed up by the legal expulsion of several Jewish leaders. At this time Cyril is revealed as at the head of dangerously volatile forces: at their head, but not always in command of them.

A similar incident occurred shortly afterwards when a Christian mob pulled one of the leading pagan critics of the Alexandrian Church from her carriage and dragged her into the church, possibly in an attempt to force her into acknowledging the Gospel. The woman in question was one of the leading philosophers of the age, the neo-Platonist Hypatia, and when she refused the threats of the mob, she was stoned to death within the church building. This scandalous murder was perpetrated by a lector of the church, and although he was not personally responsible, the finger of blame was subsequently pointed at Cyril. The event brought shame upon the whole Christian community, not only in the eyes of the pagan and Jewish elements of the city, but also from other Christian communities, who loudly criticized the behavior of the Alexandrians. After an official investigation into the riots and the murder, the numbers of the episcopal bodyguards were restricted by order of the imperial court in 416, and the archbishop was told not to interfere in civic matters.

Cyril's relations with the Byzantine Governor Orestes continued to deteriorate. But within a few years of his rebuke from the court of Constantinople all the penalties laid on him were removed and his bodyguard was increased, again by an imperial edict. This not only represents Cyril's remarkable ability to bounce back from political adversity (a factor which is more than represented in his later life), it also demonstrates the way in which the court at Byzantium recognized that it was he, not Orestes, who was the real leader of Christian Alexandria, in fact if not in theory. The imperial court was always pragmatic in such matters.

Several commentators, especially those who have wished to discredit Cyril's theology, have set these charges of racism, riot, and murder, at his door, and castigated him as a demagogue with few, if any, principles. This is to read the events naively. Life in any fifth-century Byzantine city was violent beyond the imagination and experience of most moderns, and mob violence was almost an institutionalized part of the Roman social system.[5] Emperors, city governors, and eventually Christian bishops, who assumed more and more political power from the fourth century onwards, all had to acknowledge and deal with this. Far more balanced than that caricature presented by Gibbon is the summative judgment offered by Lionel Wickham:

5 Cf. T.E. Gregory, *Vox Populi: Popular Opinion and Violence in the Religious Controversies of the fifth century* (Columbus, 1979).

"The facts are not to be denied. The picture they yield is not of a fanatical priest, hungry for power, heading a howling mob, but of an untried leader attempting, and initially failing, to master popular forces."[6]

From 412 to 418, Cyril's years on the throne of Alexandria had been turbulent enough. Thereafter his administration had a period of ten years of comparative peace, during which his hold over his church was stabilized, and his administrative control of the monasteries of Egypt was more and more established. There are several instances of Egyptian monks asking his advice. His letters to the monasteries are extant, and two of the leading monastic ascetics had close relations with him, especially the Higumen Victor, and the charismatic leader of the great monastery at Tabennesi, the thaumaturge St Shenoudi of Atripe, whom Cyril was later to take with him to the Council of Ephesus as a member of his personal entourage.

In this period of relative calm, Cyril continued his reading of the Fathers and composed doctrinal and exegetical works of considerable style and merit. They have largely been forgotten today because they were overshadowed, even in his own lifetime, by the works he composed after 428.

In that year a storm broke over the universal Church whose proportions could hardly have been envisaged by those then involved. It was a crisis that forced the whole of Christianity to examine the fundamentals of its beliefs about Jesus, and set in train no less than three ecumenical councils (Ephesus 431; Chalcedon 451; Constantinople II 553). It was Cyril's destiny to be the one who articulated a definitive vision of Christology during this time, and his works continued to dominate the decisions of ecumenical synods long after his death.

Today, as was the case in his lifetime, his work was seen in

6 L. Wickham, *Cyril of Alexandria: Select Letters* (Oxford 1983), p. xvi.

the East and West to be a standard of orthodoxy. Even his most dogged opponent, Theodoret of Cyr, came in the end to use Cyril's terminology to express his doctrine of Christ, having spent most of his life opposing Cyril himself. The theological issues that were raised at this period in the fifth century have returned with new freshness in the Church of the last two centuries, and this makes Cyril's work not only of historical or canonical significance, but of profound relevance for the contemporary understanding of the Christian tradition about the person of Jesus, God and Man. To this day Cyril of Alexandria's theology represents a definitive theological vision for Eastern Christianity's understanding of Christ, and the mystery of redemptive deification which the incarnation has effected.

In 428, few people could have seen the crisis from such a measured perspective. It began with what A. Grillmeier has called "an ecumenical scandal," as news began to spread about a new archbishop in Constantinople, his pugnacious style of doing theology, and the novel things he appeared to be saying about Christ.

A Syrian monk called Nestorius had been summoned by the emperor to assume the throne of Constantinople on the death of Sisinnius. He had been recommended by the newly appointed Archbishop John of Antioch. An outsider had been sought to break certain deadlocked factions that had formed within the capital. As might have been expected when the new archbishop was installed, he found many on all sides who did not think his face fitted. Almost at once he set to work "reforming" what he thought was a slack church.

He persuaded the emperor to restrict the races at the circus, and the numbers of dancing girls that performed there, thereby earning the hearty dislike of many of the crowds, for whom racing and exotic dancers were a consuming passion. He soon found, to his distaste, that Constantinople had evolved a new manner of monastic life in which many monastics lived within the city confines, some even working in the imperial service. Nestorius found this unacceptable and forbade them any involvement with local church or civic affairs. In doing so he alienated a large body of ascetics, several of whom were held in high regard by important and powerful aristocrats who served as their protectors. Soon after this, he forcibly closed the last Arian chapel in Constantinople. The congregation set fire to the building in defiance of his bailiffs, and the subsequent fire destroyed much property. The Byzantine military aristocracy regarded this as a highly dangerous act, unnecessary and foolish since there were many German auxiliaries then garrisoned in the city who were Arian by persuasion, and on whose loyalty the Empire needed to count.

One of Nestorius' most serious mistakes was to alienate the Augusta Pulcheria, the emperor's sister. Her power, in alliance with the monastic party, did much to cause his political downfall even before Cyril had publicly exposed his theology. Throughout the controversy, Cyril counted on the complete loyalty of his own see, as well as on buoyant international support. As for Nestorius, even from the outset his own church was divided bitterly, and the support he did command at the beginning of the crisis all too soon evaporated, leaving him exposed on every side.

Soon after Nestorius' arrival, the monastic party in Constantinople took offense at the way his team of Syrian chaplains were conducting a series of lectures on the nature of the faith. They were determined to impress on the Constantinopolitan church the teachings of the Syrian theologians Diodore of Tarsus and Theodore of Mopsuestia, who at that time were regarded in the Antiochene Patriarchate as leading theologians, but who did not command an international reputation such as Athanasius or the Cappadocian Fathers could be seen to enjoy. Diodore had approached the issue of Christology in a rather crude way that spoke of "Two Sons": one the Son of God, the other the Son of Man, the human being in whom the divine Son dwelt in an intimate association. By this way of speaking, he had hoped to solve some of the problems inherent in the interpretation of scripture which seemed to attribute divine as well as human attributes in a difficult way to the same figure of the Lord. Theodore of Mopsuestia had tempered this way of thinking, aware that the doctrine of "Two Sons," while explaining aspects of scriptural language, left the Church's belief in one Lord hopelessly compromised, but the tendency of the Antiochene theologians was to approach the issue of Christology in a way that preferred to speak of the divine Logos "associated with," or "conjoined to" the man Jesus of Nazareth.

Nestorius had tried to impose this method of theology on his church, but it met with fierce opposition from the start, from local theologians such as Proclus (later to be Archbishop of Constantinople himself) as well as from representatives of other churches, most significantly Rome and Alexandria.

Both churches kept in the capital a house for their clerics who served as local agents to the imperial court. From the beginning of the controversy Cyril was informed exactly as to what was happening. The party opposed to Nestorius objected to the way in which his chaplain had refused to allow the orthodoxy of the title "Mother of God" (Theotokos) for Mary. Following the prescripts of his Antiochene logical method, Nestorius supported his chaplain in the face of numerous complaints. He allowed that Mary could be called the Mother of God—just as she could be called the mother of the man Jesus—but that both theologies were defective since "strictly speaking" she was not the mother merely of God, or merely of a man, but the Mother of Christ, and Christ was not merely God, and not merely man, but was God conjoined to man, or if one liked, man conjoined to God.

What he thought would be a compromise again pleased no one. His method of doing theology was excessively semantic. He used the phrase " strictly speaking" time and again, and it was not long before some of his opponents had set his own hounds upon him. In 429 they appeared in the city with placards proclaiming him a heretic. They argued from the following syllogism which they deduced from their unhappy encounter with him: If Mary is not "strictly speaking" the Mother of God, then Jesus, her son, is not "strictly speaking" God. And they attributed this doctrine to their archbishop. It was not really his formulation at all, but it represented exactly what many people felt to be the "implication" of his thought.

The simple people of the city were scandalized, thinking that the archbishop was denying the divinity of Christ; others knew that, in a more complicated way, he was forcing an unacceptable christological scheme on his church with a certain amount of disingenuousness. Cyril had an eye on both factors: the necessity of correlating a highly intellectual theology with the lived experience of the ordinary Christian. At first he decided not to intervene. But news of the conflict had already reached the monasteries of Egypt causing dissensions there, and it was this that convinced him to act, and call his younger colleague to order.

He sent Nestorius letters informing him that his doctrine was defective. He also sent a dossier of Nestorius' sermons to Rome so that they could consider the case themselves. In response, Nestorius replied to Cyril with veiled threats that he might summon Cyril himself to judgment at the Church of Constantinople, and he redoubled his efforts at propagating his doctrine, now regarding those who maintained the title "Mother of God" as out and out heretics who were mythologizing the faith and "mixing up" the characteristics of deity and humanity by attributing them to the same person without distinction. Terms such as the "weariness of God" or the "flesh of God" he anathematized as wholly unacceptable confusions of terms: idiotic if not downright heretical. Much has rightly been written to the effect that few people in the course of the controversy actually listened carefully to one another (some things never change), but the row was far more than any simple misunderstanding of intent. What Nestorius regarded as the worst theological excess—the indiscriminate ascription of both divine and human attributes and characteristics to the one person—Cyril regarded as the quintessential truth revealed by the mystery of incarnation, and the very principle whereby the human race was redeemed. There were indeed radical and fundamental differences between the two schools, and with Nestorius and Cyril both claiming to speak for the authentic tradition of Christianity, an international council to test matters was inevitable. There is much evidence that Cyril had indeed considered the implications of Nestorius' doctrine very carefully. The dossier of texts that he produces from his opponent's works at the Council of Ephesus accurately reflects all that made him worried about such a theology, and it was a worry that the vast majority of bishops present at the synod shared alongside Cyril.

The events of the next three years were highly involved, but they led inexorably to a highly fractious ecumenical council, one which caused years of controversy after it, and itself initiated the agenda of three major synods following, two of which were themselves recognized as ecumenical councils defining the Church's doctrine of Christ.[7]

Nestorius was concerned that Cyril might be attempting to destabilize his church at Constantinople, using the theological dispute as an excuse. It seems that he regarded his own way of

7 For a fuller account of the history, theology, and texts: cf. J.A. McGuckin, *St Cyril of Alexandria and the Christological Controversy* (Brill, 1994).

theologizing as perfectly "traditional," and so normative that anyone who spoke in a different fashion must either be ignorant or of malicious intent. As far as Cyril was concerned, the Syrian tradition (that of Diodore and Theodore) which Nestorius was propagating at Constantinople was not a genuine tradition of the Church. In turn, he regarded it as at best a sloppy and archaic way of talking about Christ, and at worst if not heretical in essence at least tending to lead to heretical results with depressing regularity, as Diodore and Nestorius were continuing to demonstrate. Nestorius' suspicion that Cyril was only interested in attacking him for political reasons was, ironically, misplaced. He, and he alone, was responsible for the massive destabilization of his own church, especially in the way he had alienated the monks, aristocracy, and imperial ladies, so soon after his arrival. This political instability left him naked to all his enemies, especially since those among the aristocracy who were inclined to support him[8] knew all too well that in the conflict between his predecessor Sisinnius and the ascetics of Constantinople, it was the monks who had triumphed, backed as they were by the great power and influence of the Augusta Pulcheria. It was this weakness at home that also led to his mistake in underestimating Cyril's importance as a theologian.

Nestorius laid too much credence on Cyril's supposed political rivalry, and frequently dismissed his writings as if they were the badly written sermons of a pious incompetent. This was a blindspot that was to cost him dearly, for he wholly failed to read the mood of the bishops internationally, who recognized Cyril's style and method, but found that of Nestorius alien and bombastic.

As it became increasingly clear that the dissent within the Great Church was not capable of an easy resolution Nestorius

8 At first he had the ear and sympathies of the Emperor Theodosius, but his increasing loss of grip on the governance of his church alienated the Emperor from him.

suggested to the emperor that a large synod be called to adjudicate the matter. It seems that he had in mind that it should be located in Constantinople, presided over by himself as archbishop, and largely concerned to settle some matters of discipline (mainly to initiate moves against Proclus, and the pro-Cyrilline party that so vehemently opposed his theological doctrine). But Cyril had not been idle. He had written to Nestorius, and although his exchange of letters had not been well-received, his texts were destined to be given ecumenical standing at the forthcoming council as succinct summaries of the dispute. He had also composed several important treatises on the theological issues at stake. He addressed some works to the emperor, and others, separately, to the royal princesses and the empresses Pulcheria and Eudoxia, in which he collated extensive writings from the Fathers to support the case that Nestorius' doctrine was not consonant with the ancient tradition.

The Roman Church by now had also received his dossier of Nestorian texts. It had its own agents at the court of Constantinople, and through one of these, the lay theologian Marius Mercator, it had already received news that had damaged Nestorius' reputation in the eyes of Rome. One of the chief factors to earn him the Roman suspicion was the fact that he was known to have received the party of Latin bishops who had recently been synodically condemned in the West for Pelagianism. It was thought that Nestorius was contemplating reopening their case to adjudicate it afresh, a move that Rome regarded as illegitimate, in that it was a rejection of its own claim to be the supreme court of appeal for canonical investigations. When Pope Celestine received Cyril's dossier of texts relating to Nestorius' sermons, he sent them on to John Cassian in Marseilles, asking for a detailed analysis. After Cassian had eventually reported on them in the most negative terms, the Pope convened a synod in Rome and found Nestorius guilty of heresy. He demanded a recantation of doctrine, on pain of excommunication if this were resisted. Pope Celestine asked Cyril to communicate this news to Nestorius and the Eastern churches. This was something of a tacit collusion between Celestine and Cyril that ignored the canons of the Council of Constantinople in 381 designating the imperial city as the primary see in the East. Both Rome and Alexandria had resisted acknowledging these canons, and the mutual collusion of Cyril and Celestine was designed to stress the point that in the more ancient order of church affairs, it was Alexandria that had traditionally been regarded by Rome as the primary see of the East. In recognizing the veiled political rebuff when it was delivered to him, Nestorius reacted against it by disregarding the synodical process and appealing directly to the emperor.

Cyril had communicated the news to Nestorius in a "Third Letter"[9] that gave Nestorius several days in which to recant or be excommunicated by the churches of both Rome and Alexandria. This was a very serious threat indeed, but when Nestorius received it, he felt he was in a position to be able to disregard it. He had already persuaded the emperor to hold an ecumenical synod that would de facto take precedence over the local synods of Rome and Alexandria. The emperor, stirred into action by the increasing urgency of the ecclesial rifts that were growing ever wider, set the date of Pentecost 431 for the international meeting and sent out summons to the bishops of all the major churches to gather their representatives.

Nestorius' hope that the synod would meet on his home ground and under his jurisdiction was cruelly dashed, probably by the manoeuvring of the Augusta Pulcheria. When the arrangements were finally fixed, the synod was set to meet in Ephesus, a city where Nestorius was not highly regarded.

Cyril went, in advance of the date, to Ephesus from Alex-

9 Cyril's Letter 17. For available English versions of this and other central texts, see Bibliography, section A.

andria and was warmly welcomed by Memnon, the local
bishop. When Nestorius arrived in the company of the troops
from Constantinople, he was treated by the bishops already in
attendance as an excommunicate. Although he had felt capable
of disregarding the canonical sentence of Rome and Alexandria, the other bishops applied the terms of canon law strictly,
and would not allow him to function in any of the churches until
his case had been heard and adjudicated in the new synod. He
was outraged at this, but nothing would shake Cyril or Memnon
from sustaining this position. The Roman delegates were delayed on their way from the West, as was the delegation from
Syria led by John of Antioch. The latter party, which included
those bishops most likely to support Nestorius, had a long and
difficult journey to Asia Minor, and when several weeks had
passed after the date of Pentecost, and they were still several
days' journey from Ephesus, Cyril decided that he would wait
no longer.

He began to suspect that John of Antioch was deliberately
using delaying tactics to avoid having to be involved in the
ecclesiastical trial of his friend. Others have thought that Cyril
was playing the politician, wanting to begin proceedings before
the ranks of his opponents were swelled.

Both things are probably true in part. And on Sunday, June
21, 431, despite the protests from the local military supervisors,
and from the small party of Nestorius' supporters (sixteen of
them) and a larger group (over fifty) that felt Cyril was being
premature, Cyril claimed a sufficient majority (eventually rising to about 200 bishops) and declared that the synod would
delay no longer. He claimed the right, as the senior hierarch
present, to preside over the council, and also cited, as a supplementary argument for precedence, his delegation to act on
behalf of the Pope, as witnessed in Pope Celestine's letter of
the previous year.

On the following day, when matters began in earnest, Nestorius refused to answer any summons to the council. Instead his works were read out to the assembled bishops, and the relevant letters of Cyril were also read. The works of Nestorius were condemned by common acclamation, as was the custom at episcopal synods, and Cyril's letters were accepted as statements of orthodox doctrine. At the end of that long and dramatic summer's day, the crowds gathered around the Church of Mary (its remains are still visible in Ephesus today) with torches lit against the onset of night, to hear the outcome of the meeting. When it was declared that Nestorius was deposed and his doctrine anathematized, it was popularly interpreted as a victory for the Mother of God over her slanderers, and the synodical bishops were escorted back to their lodgings by torchlight, and with much rejoicing. The city that had once rung to the cry of, "Great is Diana of the Ephesians," now rang with the acclamations of Mary as the Mother of God. To the common people the honor of the Virgin had been safeguarded, and the more thoughtful among them and the bishops realized that in this title of veneration for Mary, a fundamental truth about Christ had been preserved.

A few days later, the party from Syria arrived and were enraged to hear that the synod, to which they had journeyed for so long, was over without them. John of Antioch called a counter-synod, even though its quorum of 43 bishops was but a fraction of those 200 who had met under Cyril. It declared Cyril and Memnon deposed, and all the other bishops under suspension until such time as they repented and came over to join the Syrian conventicle.

After several attempts to make an arrangement with the Syrians, the orthodox council met again and excommunicated the Syrian bishops; at which juncture the whole city was in uproar. Both sides appealed to the emperor, who finally acted by refusing any of the bishops permission to leave the city until all was resolved. He then sent out a delegate to investigate matters on the spot. By the time he arrived in Ephesus, the food supplies were running low, and several of the older hierarchs had died.

When the imperial delegate, Palladius, had noted down the events he left to report the case to the chancery back in the capital. At that point the delegates from the Pope arrived, and at another sitting of the synod they gave their support and votes to the orthodox council. When Theodosius studied the reports, however, he made the remarkable decision of upholding both parties' judgments, and held Nestorius to be deposed, but so too Cyril and Memnon. He announced his decision to uphold these sentences and exile the culprits, and then dismissed the bishops from Ephesus, probably intending to hold a smaller judicial review in Constantinople, where tempers would not run so high if it were under his personal supervision.

The emperor sent the imperial treasurer, Count John, to break this news in Ephesus, a man known to rule with a rod of iron. The bishops were duly cowed by Count John, especially when he immediately arrested Nestorius, Cyril and Memnon. But they refused to abandon the proceedings of a church synod to such blatant political control. John of Antioch acquiesced in the emperor's decision, to the disgust of several of his own contingent, but the 200 bishops who had formed Cyril's party refused to abandon their leader, especially since the whole of their doctrine had been a reaffirmation of his teaching, and they insisted that Cyril be released, demanding that their synodical decision should be recognized as the only legitimate conciliar legislation.

Count John had to return to Constantinople to report that the emperor's plan had backfired. When he came back to the capital he found it too in uproar. The news had gone out that

Nestorius had been deposed, to general rejoicing; but when the imperial heralds added that Cyril and Memnon had also been arrested and the council more or less disbanded, there was a riot. The cathedral was occupied and the message sent loud and clear, not by the crowds alone, but also by significant aristocrats and the leaders of the city's monasteries, that such an approach would not be acceptable.

Surprised by the amount of support Cyril commanded, Theodosius summoned leading members of both sides of the disputing parties to debate in his presence at the suburbs in Chalcedon. After hearing the case over several weeks, he turned more and more to favoring the Cyrilline position. Some have pointed to the fact that Cyril, from house arrest in Ephesus, arranged for lavish "presents" to be supplied to aristocrats in the capital who would plead his cause. This he certainly did, much to the chagrin of his enemies, although it was fairly common practice to accompany any legal suit in that era with what today we would regard as distasteful bribery.

What determined Theodosius' mind in the end, however, was not the money but the fact that all voices seemed to be raised for Cyril, except the tiny remnant of Syrians, who increasingly were regarded with hostility by the local people of Constantinople. Allied to this, the two hundred bishops in Ephesus, despite enduring much physical discomfort, refused to leave the city throughout that summer, even though they had been commanded to do so. They would not budge until Cyril had been released and the decrees of their council confirmed by the emperor. It was this fidelity, more than anything else, which impressed Theodosius, and led him to acknowledge the majority council as having the force of imperial law.

Knowing that he had won the day, Cyril slipped away from Ephesus in the autumn of 431 and returned triumphant to his church in Alexandria. Nestorius petitioned the emperor to return to his monastery in Antioch and was given permission to do so. The place of Nestorius was filled by a new bishop, Maximian. The Syrians, however, returned home refusing to lift their excommunication against Cyril or Memnon, and they spread the report throughout their great patriarchal territory that only their synodical meeting had been the true "Council of Ephesus," where Cyril's theology had been judged and found false.

Because they continued to regard Nestorius as having been unjustly condemned, the Syrians refused to accept the legitimacy of the new archbishop Maximian. Thus, Rome, Alexandria, and Constantinople were still out of communion with the Syrian church. It was a state of affairs that the emperor could not allow to continue, and so from the beginning of 432 the imperial court initiated a process of reconciliation aimed at bringing about a rapprochement between Cyril and John of Antioch.

It took two years, but eventually in 433 it was effected to mutual satisfaction by the exchange of a credal statement between Alexandria and Antioch, now known as the "Formula of Reunion."[10] Both sides claimed the other had backed down, and still many Syrian hardliners refused to accept the reconciliation, as did several hardliners in Cyril's own church. The former group endured until Chalcedon, and after their definitive exile then became the nucleus for the so-called "Nestorian" (Assyrian) Church, as they left imperial borders to work more and more within the boundaries of Persia. The latter group thought that Cyril had given in too much to Syrian demands that the christological doctrine should be expressed in some of their terms, and they thought that the old man was losing his grip. This Egyptian party caused Cyril much trouble in his old age, and at his death would initiate a determined movement that

10 Known in Antiquity as the "Symbolum Ephesinum." It is Cyril's Letter 39. For available translations see Bibliography, section A.

eventually rejected the Council of Chalcedon to set up a parallel "Monophysite" hierarchy.

Analysis of the Formula of Reunion shows that Cyril's estimate of the reconciliation was the truer one. He felt that he had given ground on vocabulary, but had not moved on matters of principle. He made an important distinction, which has often not been sustained by commentators since, that there was a world of difference between the authentic christology of the Syrian church, represented by John of Antioch, and the perverse christology of Nestorius, which was heretical in that it divided Christ into two. With John he would negotiate and compromise, because the faith was not at issue, but with Nestorius there could be no negotiation.

In the years after the restoration of peace, Cyril's reputation was established as the leading theologian of the Christian world. He continued to write a large body of books, including theological treatises and scriptural commentaries. In 438, the emperor asked him to accompany his estranged wife Eudoxia on her pilgrimage to Jerusalem. While he was in the holy city, he was approached by a delegation from Syria who informed him that in large areas of that patriarchate the false report of Ephesus was still in vogue, and that the writings of Diodore and Theodore of Mopsuestia, the teachers of Nestorius, were still held up as the highest theological authorities, as if the condemnation of Nestorius had meant nothing at all.

When he returned to Alexandria, Cyril determined to open the fight once more. This time he realized that unless he could definitively show these writings to be misleading and dangerous, the gains of the council of Ephesus would be in vain. To this end he set out on a concerted campaign to discredit the works of Diodore and Theodore. His task was made all the harder by the fact that these two were regarded as the leading theologian saints of Syria.

When Cyril asked the new Archbishop of Constantinople, his former ally Proclus, to assist him in this campaign, he was met with a rebuff. The emperor had asked Proclus to use all his diplomatic skill in reconciling the differences that still endured throughout the Syrian church. Proclus thought that Cyril's new offensive would make matters worse rather than better. Against his better judgment, and under considerable pressure from the court, Cyril agreed to act more circumspectly. He still wrote treatises attacking Theodore and Diodore as the "teachers and sources of Nestorius' heresy" but more and more he made his apologetic less "frontal."

Cyril's judgment on matters proved only too prophetic. Proclus did not manage, in the end, to effect a lasting solution; and it was Cyril's insight that was adopted at the Second Council of Constantinople in 553, when Justinian followed Cyril's call for a definitive rejection of these works from the canon of orthodoxy, and both Diodore and Theodore were retrospectively anathematized.

It was in his final years, when he was able to look back on the course of the whole Nestorian controversy, that Cyril composed the treatise "On the Unity of Christ."[11] It has justly been regarded as one of his most mature theological works. As well as setting out a comprehensive theological exposition of why the Syrian tradition of "Two Sons" is pernicious and cannot be accepted as an authentic tradition of the Church, Cyril takes time for several sideswipes against the continuing high regard in which the Syrian church held Diodore and Theodore.

When Cyril was writing this treatise, his archrival Nestorius had been rearrested for refusing to stop a war of pamphleteering, and he was sent first to exile in the rose-red city of Arabian Petra, and finally to a lifelong exile in the penal colony of the Great Oasis in the Saharan desert. Even then the heat of the

11 Greek title: *Oti Eis O Christos*. Latin title: *Quod Unus Sit Christus*.

controversy was far from over. It was not even a matter of the dying embers of a fire, for the whole argument would soon flare up again at the Synod of Ephesus (449), and the councils of Chalcedon (451) and Constantinople II (553). Indeed, the effects of the divisions are still visible in the church today.

At the end of his life Cyril's letters to John of Antioch and Theodoret of Cyr, who had been his most determined opponents for years, show that some real degree of personal and doctrinal reconciliation had been reached. By this time he was an old and sick man. John of Antioch died before him. Nestorius would outlive him by six or seven years.

Cyril had suffered several illnesses in the course of his life, and in 444 he took to his bed for the last time. He died on June 27, 444, a little short of his seventieth year. Almost as soon as the funeral was over, his archdeacon Dioscorus, one of those who thought he had been far too eirenic in his approach to the Syrians, initiated a purge of his family. All their involvement in the financial and political affairs of the Alexandrian Church was brought to an end, thus terminating a dynasty that Theophilus had inaugurated almost sixty years before. Dioscorus, a much less able theologian and a much less skilled politician than Cyril, was soon to lead one of the great churches of Christendom to a ruination from which it would never fully recover, before the Islamic invasions of the seventh century reduced it to a dim shadow of its former glory as an intellectual capital of the Christian world.

Alexandria was a Christian city that had (and was to continue to have) a great an honorable roll of martyrs, holy monks, and doctors of the church to ennoble its annals, but with the exception of St Athanasius it had no one as remarkable as St Cyril occupying the episcopal throne. Together with Origen and Athanasius, Cyril stands as one of the greatest theologians of the Alexandrian Church, and like his other two compatriots, one of the greatest theologians of the Universal Church's history. For all three of them, their works were not only profoundly important in themselves, but even more significant in terms of the influence they had over Christian teaching and understanding for centuries to come, and for the way in which they determined the very shape of what would, or would not be, regarded as ecumenical orthodoxy.

Cyril's feastday is celebrated on June 9 and again on January 18, in the company of St Athanasius.

His festal Troparion acclaims him in the following terms:

Hail Translucent star,
defending warrior to the Holy Virgin
who shouted out above all the hierarchs at Ephesus
that she was the Mother of God...
Rejoice most blessed Cyril,
spring of theology and
river of the knowledge of God.
Never cease to intercede with Christ on our behalf.

A Synopsis of St Cyril's Christological Doctrine
It would be no exaggeration to describe Cyril as one of the most profound and subtle of the Church's theologians. As might be expected of one who worked in an era where Christian terminology demanded an unusually acute reworking, his doctrine is both technical and philosophically demanding. One of his most important contributions to Christian history is the way in which he worked out an exact terminological scheme of discourse. It would be a mistake, however, to think that this makes Cyril a dull writer. There are passages where, like many another ancient rhetor, his capacity for elaborating an argument through several variations sometimes exceeds the patience of modern readers, but throughout all his work there is a spirit of passion and religious fervor that communicates itself to those who have the eyes to see and the ears to hear, and the Dialogue presented

here represents Cyril in the full flight of his theological maturity, yet in a literary style that is at once fluent and elegant.

Cyril is motivated by a profoundly mystical understanding
of the indwelling power of God, one that makes the incarnation
of the Logos not merely a theological nicety of dogmatic
history, but the primary way in which a Christian person
experiences the presence of the Lord and the effects of his
deifying grace. This practicality and religious spirit is visible
even in those passages where our author makes demands on the
philosophical acumen of his readers. The full complexity of his
theological doctrine, and that of Nestorius his opponent, has
been expounded in several places, and the reader may be
referred, for a fuller treatment, to the works mentioned in the
Select Bibliography. Here I will attempt merely a short sketch
of his general christological doctrine, with a minimum of
technical and historical digressions.

As far as Nestorius was concerned, language about the incarnation had to retain a primary sense of the difference between deity
and humanity: both that distance between God and his creatures,
and that between the divine and the human aspects of the Christ.
Once language had established the respective differences, the
Christian mind could appreciate the closeness of a God who, in
the person of Jesus Christ, entered into association with human-
kind. If Nestorius' scheme was a little woolly on the critical
question of whether this man (Jesus) was or was not God,[12] then
at least, as he saw it, it was a scheme that insisted on the full
integrity of all the elements that comprised it: God and the creature
were radically different, Jesus was fully human in every respect

12He regarded the question posed as too crude to be given a direct
  answer—but that did not stop his critics, then or now, from asking it
  of him, and sensing that the question was too critical simply to be
  dismissed as illicit because of its clumsiness of phrasing. For a fuller
  elaboration of Nestorius' doctrine cf. McGuckin, 1988, 1994.

including human limitations of consciousness, psychology and power, while the divine Logos was fully God, untrammelled by the human body of Jesus. For Nestorius, the human life of Jesus was something that the Logos was in communion with, not one that dominated or subjugated him in any way.

Cyril's instinct on the incarnation ran counter to this. He found the notion of the Logos' "association" with a man to be abhorrent to Christian tradition on two grounds: First, it made for little distinction between Jesus and one of the ancient prophets who could also be said to have God inspiring them, or "indwelling" them; second, it did not convey enough of the power and intimacy of the "Union" between divinity and humanity, or its effects on human nature, which Cyril saw to be the very heart and central purpose of the whole scheme of the incarnation. In short, for Cyril the primary message of the incarnation was not about the discrete relationship of God and man, but nothing less than the complete reconciliation of God and Man in Jesus.

Cyril consistently opposed the keyword of "Union" (*Henosis*) to that of the Antiochenes who used "Association." Cyril insisted that the incarnation is not for the sake of God, but for the redemption of the human race. As such, it is an "economy," or practical scheme, that is meant to do something. In the incarnation, God is at work among creatures, not merely playacting on the stage of the world, and that work is a mysterious but inexorable transformation of the human life of his disciples into something radically new. This aspect of dynamic transformation (*Theosis*) is something critical in Cyril's thought; it is, indeed, its main pillar, and those who have accused Cyril of being too cavalier in his attitude to Jesus' real experience of human life, have largely failed to appreciate his point: that the divine Lord truly experiences all that is genuinely human, in order to transform that which is mortal into the immortal.

Cyril understands that the incarnation of God as man is not a static event, but rather the pattern and archetype of a process. He points to the seamless union of God and man in the single divine person of Jesus, truly God and man at one and the same time, founded on the single subjectivity of Christ, as not merely a sacrament of the presence of God among us, but a sacrament of how our own human lives are destined to be drawn into his divine life, and transformed in a similar manner. In short, for Cyril the manner of the incarnation is analogous to the manner of the sanctification and transfiguration of Christ's disciples.

This process of transformation was referred to by the Alexandrian theologians as "deification" (*Theosis*). As Sts Irenaeus and Athanasius had succinctly put it centuries earlier: "He (the Word) became man, that man might become god." In his turn Cyril teaches that "What he was by nature, we become by grace." Theosis does not signify a pagan conception of becoming divine, which would be either crass mythologism or one of the worst excesses of Nietzschean arrogance, but on the contrary denotes something radically different and biblically founded-something that the Western Church approached through its theological doctrines of Atonement and Beatific Vision.

Cyril had in mind that when the divine Logos became incarnated he summoned his church to a new style of being, a new theandric destiny. Before the incarnation, "divine" and "human" signified ontologically different categories of being. A vast chasm existed between the creature and the Creator, not only morally, but existentially. After the incarnation, the order of being (God's ordering of the terms of the universe) has been radically altered. In the incarnation, two realities which were philosophically and theologically impossible to combine, have been demonstrably united in Christ. This union is impossible, but it is nonetheless accomplished as a simple act of God's infinite power; the invisible Lord is now made visible, the

Immaterial One is made flesh, he who cannot be limited accepts the limitations of an earthly life, the Immortal One comes willingly to his own death. Cyril loves to apply such strong paradoxes of language. The antitheses give his thought a religious drive and vigor which he knows well how to put to effect in preaching. He accuses Nestorius of being too ready to judge what is or is not fitting for God by the terms of human logic, which he has mistakenly elevated as an absolute indicator of truth. As Cyril sees it, he has forgotten that human logic is flawed because of sinfulness and the limited vision consequent on our corruption. The argument over theological method was very intense between Cyril and Nestorius, and in turn moved into an important debate over the right interpretation of scriptural texts. In both instances, Cyril resisted the application of logic alone as a guide to the Christian mind, and appealed to a sense of tradition as manifesting a common inner spiritual experience through several generations of theologian-saints.

But in spite of his appeal to represent traditional belief, does not his language involve the Church in a semi-pagan concept of God, where, like Zeus, a divinity can descend to earth and change his form to live in a physical fashion? Far from it, Cyril argued. The incarnation does not limit or remove the infinite power of God, it is itself simply an expression or act of that infinite power, one which presses the limits of our understanding, but which is not contradictory or illogical (as Nestorius had accused him of being). To imagine that the Logos' divine omnipotence is compromised by the human life he now leads is to regard him as having "laid aside" his deity when he became man. Cyril rejects this conception and argues that he who was eternal God became man while ever remaining what he was, that is eternal God.

But was this, in turn, merely to make theology a meaningless conundrum? or make the human life of the divine Jesus merely a pretense, or a factor all but wiped out in the face of the overwhelming presence of a deity taking it over? Cyril argued that this followed only for those who had failed to understand that the incarnation was fundamentally a time-bound act of rescue for the human race, one that had to be contextualized in a larger scheme of God's eternal philanthropy and providence for the world. The physical incarnation was a specific divine philanthropy of healing addressed to physical creatures, and meant to have an effect that began at physical level and brought material creaturehood back up into a divine communion that transcended material capacity, while never eschewing materiality. This position of being a transcendently immanent creature was for Cyril a mystery, but not an illogicality—on the contrary, a promise held out to the world in the doctrine of the glorified resurrection body.

As Cyril saw it, divine power in the incarnate Lord did not strive to express itself in contradistinction, or in opposition, to other forms of life (including human consciousness), but on the contrary was the very context which allowed all other lifeforms to subsist and develop. For Cyril, then, the deity and humanity were not like two weights on a pair of scales, poised in an uneasy balance in Christ; rather the one was the nurturing matrix of the other. Just as the deity of Christ did not suppress or falsify his own humanity, so Cyril understood it to be paradigmatic that, for the redeemed person, union with God would not cramp individuality but rather liberate personhood and enhance it. As far as Cyril was concerned, even an ordinary human life exhibited at its heart a sense of spiritual yearning and transcendence which often tried to employ its material condition as part of its spiritual ascent—or, put another way, to express its spiritual identity through its material consciousness. For Cyril, what was true of the whole race, that it ontologically subsisted within the orbit of God's powerful presence, was most particularized in the case of the Christ, whose humanity was a unique, direct, and personal expression of the divine presence.

Cyril took the image of a dual capacity, spirit animating flesh (the soul in the body) as an example of how he conceived the union of God and man in Christ. The Godhead lives without restriction in the incarnate form, just as it enjoys omnipotence in its eternal state, before the incarnation. Once within the incarnation, however, the divine Logos lives by choice within the human material conditions of incarnated life. The two modes of life are like the proximity of soul and body in an ordinary human being.

In the case of an ordinary person, the different "natures" of both realities does not preclude their union, nor does it demand that both entities be reduced to one or the other; on the contrary both can have integrity while at the same time enjoying an integral union that allows new conditions and new possibilities of existence to flourish. From the very fact of the union of body and soul Cyril points out how a human being results. For Cyril the full deity of the Word unites with a perfect human existence and from the intimacy of that spiritual and material union, the one Christ results.

Cyril felt that the soul-body image was the best attempt he could make to depict an irreducibly mysterious reality of the divine human relation within Christ, one he saw as a uniquely personal act of God. He offers supplementary images for the relationship in the form of the lily and its perfume, the fire within a coal, a jewel and its radiance. What he was searching for was a concept of natural interpenetration where the two realities (e.g., deity and humanity) both subsisted perfectly intact, but not in any parallel association, rather in a dynamic interpenetration and mutuality that effected new conditions and possibilities by virtue of that intimate union. This was why he was very anxious to insist that the Word of God, deity in all its fullness, united with a human existence. The Word did not unite with a man, but with humanity. What this means is that he wished to avoid any sense that there was a human being (Jesus, a Jewish rabbi from Nazareth) alongside a divinity (The Word of God), or any suggestion that a man was seized by the Spirit of God, in the way the Adoptionist heresy of earlier centuries had taught. But what does it mean to say that the Word united with humanity? Is it not a fundamentally abstract conception ill suited to express so personal a theological mystery?

For Cyril the criticism did not follow at all. He regarded humanity as a way of being, a manner of expressing identity in and through the material circumstances of bodily life. He did not define humanity as personal being per se. In other words he distinguished personhood both from the condition in which personhood arose, and from the manner in which it was expressed. If, as he would argue, even ordinary human beings could never be reduced in their spiritual identities merely to that bodily condition, so it was (and even more so) for the Word of God Incarnate. His person was divine and could not be reduced to the bodily life, yet it elected to express itself through that bodily manner. As a result even the bodily life became a direct vehicle of the revelation of the divine.

Cyril knew that at the center of this vision lay a great and serious question over his understanding of the subjective unity of Christ. If he rejected the whole of the Nestorian scheme as being too divisive of Christ's personal unity (he accused it of inevitably suggesting "Two Sons," or a man Jesus alongside a divine Logos) then how did he himself account for Christ's inner subjectivity?

This was the key question of all his writings after 428, and it is a dominant idea within the present treatise, supplying its central thesis as the very title of the work: "On the Unity of Christ." His task was not an easy one. The prior tradition had suggested ways of approach but not clearly defined them. In addition, Cyril's generation had come to the point of crossroads between two very disparate theologies, both of which had proved, or were proving, unacceptable to Orthodox consensus: the Syrian doctrine of Two Sons, and the Apollinarist doctrine which accounted for the subjective unity of Christ by teaching that the divine Logos dispensed with a human mind or consciousness in Christ, because the superior displaced the inferior. The latter position had rightly been rejected as a poor account of the incarnation that turned out to be a destruction of humanity, not an assumption of it.

Cyril knew that his task lay in a different direction to both extremes. He had to account for the integrity of the deity and the humanity while demonstrating their integral communion, and the results of it. He settled on the key term of "Union" (*Henosis*). From deity and humanity a union has taken place; not an overlap, or a co-habitation, or a relationship, or a displacement, or an association. None of the things his opponents had proposed. He argued for a union in the strict sense of the word, yet a union that was of the type that did not destroy its constituent elements. It was thus in the manner of the soul-body union in humans, a union that effected new conditions and capacities for both constituents while preserving their basic elements intact, and not, for example, in the manner of a union of sand and sugar (one that did nothing to either element and did not really combine either part for any positive end), or a union of fire and wood (one which only worked by destroying the basis of the elements so united).

In the case of Christ, Cyril speaks of this union of deity and humanity as a "Hypostatic Union." The person of the Logos is the sole personal subject of all the conditions of his existence, divine or human. The Logos is, needless to say, the sole personal subject of all his own acts as eternal Lord (the creation, the inspiration of the ancient prophets, and so on), but after the incarnation the same one is also the personal subject directing all his actions performed within this time and this space, embodied acts which form the context of the human life of Christ in Palestine. The phrase "the selfsame" recurs time and again in his writings as a way of insisting on this doctrine of single-subjectivity as the keystone of the entire Christology debate. Cyril would undoubtedly argue that Christ was fully human in every possible sense, but in the twentieth century new problems have arisen over his understanding of what that might mean, for today, and in this we are unlike all the ancient protagonists of all sides, since we tend to see the whole issue of subjectivity and personhood in terms drawn from the analytical psychology of the nineteenth and twentieth centuries. Accordingly, we approach the notion and the problem insofar as it impinges on the doctrine of incarnation, in terms of what could be called "psychic consciousness."

Cyril, however, would refuse to reduce the notion of person to those psychic experiences. For him, personhood (either in the case of Jesus, or in the case of humans in general) was not a product of a material based consciousness but, on the contrary, consciousness was the effect of a divinely created personhood. Modern psychology finds this perspective a difficult one to assimilate, but Cyril was adamant in rejecting the Aristotelian empiricist view that identity was reducible to brain act. He approached personhood as a god-given and transcendent mystery, with the full destiny of such an identity lying in another age and another condition: the Kingdom of God.

For Cyril, then, there was only one personal subject, and one personal reality in Christ, and that was the divine Logos. But Christ was not simply the Logos of God, he was the Logos as he had chosen to enter fully into human life; and in so far as the Logos lived a human life, directly and personally, within all the historical and material limitations imposed by the lifeform (constricts that applied within his life in history as man, but not within his co-terminous life outside time as God), then Christ was at once divine and human-inseparably so. Cyril regarded this "at once" as a synchronized enjoyment of two life-forms, neither of which prevented the terms of the other, but both of which were enhanced by the intimate experience provided by the other. In other words, neither the deity or humanity of Christ was diminished by the incarnation, but both were, in a real sense, "developed" by the experience: the humanity ontologically and morally so, the divinity economically so.

His critics wanted elaboration of what this enhancement meant. An "enhancement" after the manner of Apollinaris was not regarded as acceptable at all. Cyril argued that this was far from the only way of depicting the benefits the divine presence conferred on the human nature of Jesus. He drew, instead, a picture of Jesus' humanity which was suffused with the divine light and graciousness: a divinization of the flesh of Christ which rendered it uniquely powerful and health-giving, while remaining essentially human flesh. The fact that Christ's touch conferred healing was explained by Cyril on the basis that it was the human finger of none other than God, and therefore human flesh, but by no means ordinary human flesh-rather the life-giving flesh of God.[13] He was thus presenting an image of something that remained integral (or intact) but not unchanged, on the contrary enhanced. To those who would argue that this "change" destroyed the essential human condition, Cyril argued rather that it fulfilled the essential human condition, whose destiny was not to resist divine transfiguration but to be summoned to an ever deepening communion with God's trans-

13 Cyril's eucharistic arguments are very important in this regard, and follow up this central insight sacramentally. Cf. Chadwick (1951) and Gebremedhin (1977).

forming grace. This is why Cyril saw the Logos' enhancement of Jesus' flesh as the first-fruits of his transformation of the humanity of all disciples. For Cyril, the incarnation was a fundamental "process" of such transformation.

If this explains how the deity can enhance the humanity, how could it possibly be said that humanity can enhance divinity? Nestorius accused Cyril particularly on this point, arguing that his way of thinking could only lead to a reduction of the status and capacity of the deity. To this Cyril developed on what he meant by the divinity's "economy of salvation." Cyril argued that while the deity considered in itself (that is considered outside the incarnation, and outside time or space), could never change, since it was already absolute and perfect, this did not mean that the deity could never act in different ways: otherwise there would be no relationship between God and his creation. God acted within time and space, not because this was his own way of acting, but because it was his creation's way, and for the sake of his philanthropic relation to the world God was prepared to perform the impossible: the Timeless One engages with history. For Cyril, if one denied that, one denied the whole validity of a Creator God who worked out his covenant with the human race within history. In the case of the incarnation, the same paradox was witnessed again, yet in a more intimately unique manner. The incarnation, as Cyril saw it, was an act of omnipotent power, in which the eternal Lord directly and personally chose to experience the conditions of an historical and material life. If that life was a mere sham, Cyril says, and he did not really experience limitation, doubt, suffering, and all the knocks and blows that human life is prey to, then why bother to engage in the incarnation at all? The answer, for Cyril, is not far behind—he chose to engage personally in all the range of human experience in order to set new terms for the transfiguration of that condition. In particular, Cyril discusses human suffering and death.

He used a recurrent phrase which his opponents pilloried, interpreting it as an indication that Cyril did not take Christ's human experience seriously; he spoke of how Christ "suffered impassibly" (*apathos epathen*). The catchiness of the slogan was typical of Cyril's apologetic style, and as with other catch-phrases he chose terms that most shockingly set out the lines of his thought while flatly contradicting the main premises of his opponents. In other words, the phrase is a densely apologetic one that has to be carefully unpacked in order to appreciate what he meant by it. One thing is unarguable, Cyril is no docetic who is denying the reality of Christ's sufferings. On the contrary, he points to the whole experience of incarnation as adding a unique aspect to the divinity: the personal experience of human suffering and death. This "adding to" the deity is impossible if considered in terms of natures: divine nature cannot be added to or subtracted from in terms of its essence; but it is possible, Cyril argues, in terms of personal experience of a lifeform. And in the incarnation Cyril sees the eternal God directly experiencing suffering and death— insofar as like other men he too is brought under the terms of the human lifeform.

Cyril sees this part of the incarnate transaction as the key of redemption. For although God experiences suffering and death, just as he experiences all other human factors,[14] he does not become dominated by suffering or death. It is the same with his deity as with his humanity: the conditions of the one do not wipe out the distinct realities of the other, even though there is a dynamic mutual experience passing between the two.

Cyril presses this point home with a decisive move of language that has since become known as the doctrine of the "Exchange of Properties," or the "Communication of Idioms"

14Like the other Fathers, Cyril excludes the experience of sin from Jesus, something which he sees as not essentially "human" in any case, merely a perversion of true humanity.

(*Antidosis Idiomatum*). He argued passionately that, on the basis of this direct personal mutuality of experience founded on the single divine personality of the Logos who enjoyed both conditions or lifeforms, it was permissible to attribute the experiences of both natures to one and the same person-always understanding that one's language referred to the incarnate condition. And so Cyril pressed his point home in his usual graphic and paradoxical linguistic style: God wept. God died. God sat upon the Virgin's lap and suckled. To his opponents, especially Nestorius, this language broke the very foundations of their christological scheme, and they attacked it vehemently as akin to mythology. For Cyril, it was the one truth (that the divine Logos was the only personal subject experiencing all the acts of the incarnation) that saved the doctrine of incarnation from mythology, and at the same time explained why the incarnation was necessary. Before the incarnation the Immortal God could not possibly die, in any sense of the words. Now, in the conditions of the incarnation, it is perfectly true to say that God has willingly died, yet being God has burst the chains of death in the very act of submitting to them.

This redemptive system of exchange and transformation in Cyril is called "Appropriation Theory," and it is in some senses the very heart of his christological argument. Whenever he insists, as he does time and time again, on pressing the logic of phrases like "the death of God," or "the Mother of God," it is this wider theological construct he is invoking. This is why, as has often been said, Cyril's robust defence of the title of Theotokos was at heart a christological and soteriological statement rather than a statement about Mariology per se. Apart from the use of this form of "Exchange of Properties" language, Cyril also applies a favorite phrase, "One Incarnate Nature of God the Word," to sum up and signify the transactive element at the heart of the incarnation. Like his other terms, this was deliberately designed as a "tweaking of the nose" of his opponents. Some critics have suggested that this manner Cyril had of using such loud colors in his apologetic pallet made the controversy more lurid than it needed to have been. It was Cyril's opinion that only such stark terms were capable of forcing his opponents out from a bland theological vagueness that covered up their essentially unacceptable premises. His contemporary opponents, such as Nestorius, Theodoret of Cyr, Andrew of Samosata, and others in the Syrian patriarchate, simply read them as examples of extreme Apollinarist heresy. In this they were wrong. There are grounds for thinking that there is some truth in both the other two views expressed: that Cyril made the argument sharper and faster than it might otherwise have been, and that perhaps there was a negative as well as a positive side to that.

It is much the same when we consider his treatment of Nestorius as an opponent. It is certainly the case that Cyril was doggedly opposed to all Nestorius stood for, and that he might not have read his opponents' works with due regard to the subtlety of their argument on every occasion. There are no grounds, however, for thinking that Cyril did not understand Nestorius' theology. What he felt to be at stake was an underlying tendency that disturbed him greatly. If he was not ready to compromise over the doctrinal disagreement with Nestorius, seeing it turn on the fundamental issue of single subjectivity, this does not mean to say that he was a rigid or intransigent thinker. When he was convinced that the central issue was safe, he was quite prepared to go the extra mile to meet the Syrian theologians' points. It was his willingness to compromise when the central facts had been established, that cost him some popularity at home in his final years.

Over the last century, in our own time, the issues for which he fought so passionately, the subjectival unity of the incarnate

Lord, and the difference between the Christian theology of incarnation and pagan mythological schemes of religion, have once again come into large scale dispute. This has caused considerable christological revision in the Western churches, and it is not surprising to see a concomitant review of Nestorian theology in the process and (one might deduce) something of an attempt to revive it in terms of popular dogmatics. It is certainly the case that, in the European literature of the last hundred years Cyril has been denigrated both as a thinker and as a person, in ways that suggest unspoken doctrinal battles are being waged behind the front of historical scholarship. In several influential modern studies, the Antiochene tradition which Cyril attacked (that of Diodore, Theodore, and Nestorius) has been offered as a legitimate and ancient part of an authentically pluralist Christian vision, and Cyril has been censured as one who arrogantly crushed it. Given that these old arguments are far from dead, and given the importance of the debate in terms of what constitutes the Church's doctrine of Christ, and how it articulates its authentic tradition, then it should prove both opportune and instructive to present this translation of Cyril to a new generation of readers. It is one of Cyril's most elegant and approachable writings, and explains at the end of a long battle from which he has emerged successful, why in his own time he utterly rejected such a relativistic and inclusive approach to the nature of Christian Paradosis— that "Tradition" of Christianity which is not merely a historico-theological matter, but an enduring question of the articulation of the church's spiritual experience of its redeeming Lord.

ON THE UNITY OF CHRIST[1]

A. People of true and good sense, who have intellectually gathered that knowledge which gives life, are never jaded by the sacred sciences. Indeed it is written that: "Man shall not live by bread alone, but by every word that comes from the mouth of God" (Mt 4:4; Dt 8:3). The word of God is food for the mind and a spiritual "bread that strengthens the heart of man," as the Book of Psalms sings (cf. Ps 104:15).

B. How right you are.

A. The wise and eloquent men among the pagans are full of admiration for a well-turned phrase. One of their main preoccupations is with elegance of expression. They are filled with the greatest enthusiasm for good style, and take great pride in verbal dexterity. The base material of their poets is merely lies fashioned in rhythms and meters for grace and harmony, but for the truth they have little if any regard. I would say that they are sick from the lack of any true or proper notion of the nature and reality of God. Or rather, as the most holy Paul puts it: "They have been mistaken in their reasonings and their insensible hearts are darkened. Thinking themselves wise, they have become as fools, and have exchanged the glory of the incorruptible God for the likeness of an image of corruptible

1 Texts: *Quod Unus Sit Christus*, PG 75:1253-1361; Ed. P.E. Pusey, *Works of S. Cyril* vols. 1-7 (Oxford, 1868) (Vol.7, pp. 334-424); ed. G. M. de Durand, *Deux Dialogues Christologiques*, Sources Chrétiennes, 97, pp. 302-514 (Paris, 1964). The treatise seems, by its maturity of thought and assured tone, to be one of the last works Cyril wrote on the Nestorian controversy, at a time when his apologetic had moved more towards opposing the continued influence of Diodore of Tarsus. It could be dated circa 438.

man, and birds, and beasts and reptiles" (Rom 1:21-23).

B. Quite so. And God said of them through the voice of Isaiah: "Know that their hearts are but dust, and that they have erred" (Is 44:20).

A. Then so much for them. As for the inventors of impure heresies, those profaners and apostates who have opened their mouths wide against the divine glory, "those who have uttered perverted things" (Acts 20:30), we could accuse them of having slipped in their madness as low as the foolish pagans, perhaps even lower, for it would have been better never to have known the way of truth than once to have known it to have turned away from the sacred commandment which was handed on to them. What the Book of Proverbs so rightly speaks of has indeed come about: "that the dog has returned to its vomit, and no sooner has it washed than the pig returns to wallow in the slime" (Pr 26:11; 2 Pet 2:21-22). They have circulated among themselves blasphemous accusations against Christ, and like wild ferocious wolves they ravage the flock for which Christ died. They pillage what is his very own "bloating themselves on what is not theirs," as it is written (Hab 2:6 LXX), and "stuffing their gorge to the full." How aptly does that saying apply to them, that "They came out from us but were not part of us" (1 Jn 2:19).

B. Indeed they were not.

A. Well, this is an opportunity for us to consider the doctrine of such people. Some are foolish enough to bring down the Word and Only Begotten Son of God from his supreme station. They reduce him from equality with God the Father by denying his consubstantiality and refusing to crown him with a perfect identity of nature.[2]

2 The Arians. Note how Cyril immediately goes on to characterise the Nestorian position in the following sentence, as something that is logically akin to Arianism. The elision of heresies was a patristic "topos" in the 5th century, but Cyril's insistence on the point suggests this was his truly held logical analysis of Nestorianism.

Others more or less retrace the same path as those we have just mentioned. They fall into the snares of death and "into the pit of hell" (Pr 9:18 LXX) as they pervert the mystery of the fleshly economy of the Only Begotten, teaching a folly which is in a way the twin of that of their predecessors. In effect the first group, insofar as lies within their power, drag down the Word born of God the Father from the heights of divinity even before his incarnation, while the second group have decided to wage war against the Word even in his incarnation. These shameless people even dare to criticize his loving grace towards the human race, for they think that the fact that he inflicted flesh upon himself and took up the limitations of this self-emptying, that is, became man and "appeared on earth and engaged with men" (Bar 3:38) even though he was God by nature and seated with the Father, all shows a lack of good sense.

B. How rightly you put it.

A. Nonetheless, God-inspired scripture will cry out against both forms of madness. It acts as the ambassador of truth and shows up the feeble and shameful system of these people. It establishes in the paths of the Godhead all those who are accustomed to fix the eyes of their mind with care and subtlety upon this mystery. Still I would like to question you about these people who have wickedly debased the venerable and ineffable economy of the Savior. Certainly this matter seems to disturb you somewhat?

B. You discern correctly, "for I have been consumed with zeal for the Lord" (1 Kg 19:10), and have been so put out by all this that I am deeply disturbed. And I feel afraid when I look to where their teaching will end, for they have adulterated the faith that was handed on to us by the inventions of that serpent so recently appeared, injecting their frigid, perverted, and idiotic notions like venom into the souls of the simple.

A. But tell me, please, who is this serpent who has so

recently appeared? And what are these idiotic things he sets against the teachings of the truth?

B. The serpent so recently appeared is that crooked one whose tongue is drunk on venom. Not only does he not welcome the tradition of all the initiates throughout the world (or rather that of all the God-inspired scriptures), but he even innovates as seems fit to him, and denies that the holy virgin is the Mother of God, and calls her Christ-Mother instead, or Mother-of-the-Man, not to mention the other shocking and absurd ideas he introduces to the orthodox and pure teachings of the catholic Church.

A. You speak of Nestorius, I think. I am already somewhat familiar with his thought but as to its precise nature, my friend, I am not so sure. How can he say that the holy virgin is not the Mother of God?

B. He maintains it is because she has not given birth to God, since the Word was before her, or rather is before every age and time being coeternal with God the Father.

A. In that case it is clear that they must also deny that Emmanuel is God; and so it would seem that the evangelist interpreted the term pointlessly when he said, "And being translated this means God-with-us" (Mt 1:23; Is 7:14). And yet, because he is God made man, this is exactly how we ought to name the one that is born of the holy virgin according to the flesh, as God the Father clearly teaches through the voice of the prophet.

B. But this is not how it appears to these people. They say that God, or rather the Word of God, has been with us in the form of helping us. For he saved everything under heaven through the one that was born of a woman.

A. But tell me, was he not with Moses delivering the Israelites from the land of Egypt and from their tyranny, as it is written: "With strong hand and outstretched arm"? (Ps 136:12). And after this do we not find him saying to Joshua quite clearly: "As I was with Moses so shall I be with you"? (Jos 3:7).

B. This is true.

A. Then why are neither of them called Emmanuel? Why does this name apply only to the one who was so wondrously born of a woman, according to the flesh, in these last times of the world?

B. Then how should we understand that God was born of a woman? Does it mean that the Word took up his being in her and from her?

A. Away with such a horrid and vile opinion. These are the teachings of a wanderer, of a sick mind that has strayed where it should not have gone so as to think that the ineffable being of the Only Begotten could ever be the fruit of flesh. On the contrary, as God he was ineffably begotten by nature from the Father and was coeternal with him. For those who wish to know clearly how, and in what manner, he appeared in a form like our own, and became man, the divine evangelist John explains when he says: "And the Word became flesh and dwelt among us, and we beheld his glory, glory as of the Only Begotten of the Father, full of grace and truth" (Jn 1:14).

B. But they maintain that if the Word became flesh he no longer remained the Word, but rather ceased to be what he was.

A. This is nothing but foolishness and stupidity, the frenzy of a crazed mind. It seems that they are of the opinion that the term "became," inevitably and necessarily signifies change or alteration.

B. They say that this is the case, and they support their teaching on the basis of the God-inspired scriptures themselves. For he maintains that it is said somewhere about Lot's wife that: "She became a pillar of salt" (Gen 19:26); and again about Moses' staff that: "He threw it upon the ground and it became a serpent" (Ex 4:3); and that in all these cases a change of nature took place.

A. Well then, when people sing in the psalm: "And the Lord became my refuge" (Ps 94:22), and again: "O Lord you have become my refuge from one generation to the next" (Ps 90:1); what will they say about this? Has the one of whom we sing laid aside his being as God and through some transformation passed over into becoming a refuge? Has he changed by nature into something else which at first he was not?

B. Surely this approach is incongruous and unfitting to one who is God by nature. Immutable by nature, he remains that which he was and is for ever, even if one says that "he became a refuge" for various people.

A. What you have said is excellent, and perfectly true. So when we are considering God, if one uses the word "became" is it not altogether impious and absurd for someone to presume that it signifies change, rather than trying to understand it in another manner, applying some wisdom and turning instead to what is much more fitting and applicable to the unchangeable God?

B. If we are to preserve the immutability and unalterability as innate and essential to God, in what sense, then, should we say that the Word has become flesh?

A. The all-wise Paul, steward of His mysteries and sacred minister of the Gospel proclamations, explains this for us when he says, "Let each of you have among yourselves that same mind which was in Christ Jesus who, though he was in the form of God, did not count equality with God a thing to be grasped, but emptied himself, assuming the form of a slave, coming in the likeness of men; and being found in fashion as a man he humbled himself becoming obedient even to death, death on a cross" (Phil 2:5-8). And indeed, the Only Begotten Word, even though he was God and born from God by nature, the "radiance of the glory, and the exact image of the being" of the one who begot him (Heb 1:3), he it was who became man. He did not change himself into flesh; he did not endure any mixture or blending, or anything else of this kind. But he submitted himself to being emptied and "for the sake of the honor that was set before him he counted the shame as nothing" (Heb 12:2) and did not disdain the poverty of human nature. As God he wished to make that flesh which was held in the grip of sin and death evidently superior to sin and death. He made it his very own, and not soulless as some have said, but rather animated with a rational soul, and thus he restored flesh to what it was in the beginning. He did not consider it beneath him to follow a path congruous to this plan, and so he is said to have undergone a birth like ours, while all the while remaining what he was. He was born of a woman according to the flesh in a wondrous manner, for he is God by nature, as such invisible and incorporeal, and only in this way, in a form like our own, could he be made manifest to earthly creatures. He thought it good to be made man and in his own person to reveal our nature honored in the dignities of the divinity. The same one was at once God and man, and he was "in the likeness of men" (Phil 2:7) since even though he was God he was "in the fashion of a man" (Phil 2:8). He was God in an appearance like ours, and the Lord in the form of a slave. This is what we mean when we say that he became flesh, and for the same reasons we affirm that the holy virgin is the Mother of God.

B. Would you like us to compare their arguments to yours, and undertake a more profound examination of these matters, or should we simply accept your word that the question has been fully treated?

A. In my opinion the argument is faultless, spoken with wisdom and learning, and in full accord with the God-inspired scriptures. But by all means speak your mind, because a counter argument may produce some useful results.

B. Well, they say that the divine Paul writes about the Son as if he had become a curse and sin, for he says: "He who did not know sin, became sin for our sakes" (2 Cor 5:21); and again: "Christ redeemed us from the curse of the Law when he became a curse for us" (Gal 3:13). But they would maintain that this does not mean he really became a curse and sin, rather that here the holy scripture clearly means something else. In exactly the same way, they argue, we should understand the phrase: "And the Word became flesh" (Jn 1:14).

A. It is true that he has introduced this opinion that just as one says, "He became curse and sin," so in the same way did he "become flesh," and this notion holds a predominant place among his followers.

B. What do you mean? For when one says of him: "He who knew not sin became sin for our sakes and redeemed from the curse of the Law those who were under the law, becoming a curse for their sakes," then how could anyone doubt that this clearly refers to the time when the Only Begotten was incarnate and made man?

A. Well, when one speaks of the incarnation one also implies all those other things that are economically brought to bear on the one who willingly suffered this "emptying out," as for example hunger and tiredness. How could he who has all power ever have been tired, or how could one ever say that he who is the food and life of all beings was ever hungry, if he had not appropriated to himself a body which by its very nature was subject to hunger and tiredness? In the same way one could never have counted him among the lawless (for this is what it means to say that he became sin) nor would he ever have become a curse, enduring the cross for our sakes, if he had not become flesh, that is incarnated and made man for our sake, submitting to a birth like our own, although it was from a holy virgin.

B. I agree. Your opinion is right.

A. Moreover it is foolishness to think or to affirm that the Word became flesh in just the same way as he became curse and sin.

B. Tell me why.

A. Did he not become accursed in order to lift the curse? And did not the Father make him sin in order that he might bring sin to an end?

B. They too would agree with this.

A. In that case, if it is true that the Word became flesh in exactly the same way that he became curse and sin, which is how they understand it, then surely he must have become flesh for the suppression of flesh? But how would this serve to exhibit the incorruptibility and imperishability of flesh which he achieved, first of all in his own body? For he did not allow it to remain mortal and subject to corruption, thus allowing the penalty of Adam's transgression to continue to pass on to us, but since it was his own and personal flesh, that of the incorruptible God, he set it beyond death and corruption.

B. How well you put it.

A. Somewhere holy scripture says that that the first man, that is Adam, was made "a life-giving soul," while the last man, that is Christ, was made "a life-giving spirit" (1 Cor 15:45). Should we say, therefore, that as he became curse and sin for the destruction of that curse and sin, just so he became a life-giving spirit in order to suppress the state of being a living soul? These people nonsensically twist the significance of the word "became" and then maintain that he became flesh in the same way as he became curse and sin. This is the way that the incarnation, or rather the enmanment of the Word, is destroyed. For if this approach is taken as the truth then the whole sense of the mystery is lost to us; for Christ is not born, neither did he die, neither was he raised, in accordance with the scriptures. In this event where is the faith? that "word of faith which we proclaim" (Rom 10:8)? How did God raise him from the dead if he did not die? And how could he die if he had not been born according to the flesh? And "if Christ is not raised" (1 Cor 15:17) then where is that resuscitation of the dead which inspired in the saints the hope of everlasting life? And where is that revitalization of human bodies which is achieved by participation in his holy flesh and blood?

B. This is why we affirm that the Word became flesh in regard to that generation from a woman, according to the flesh, which is said to have taken place in the last times of this present age, even though, as God, he exists before every age.

A. Exactly so. For it was in this way that he "became like us in all things except sin" (Heb 4:15). The all-wise Paul bears witness to this when he says: "Since the children have a common share in flesh and blood he himself equally participated in these things so that through his death he could reduce to powerlessness the one who held the dominion of death, that is the devil, and that he might liberate those who all their lives were held in slavery by the fear of death. For he did not take his descent from the angels, rather from Abraham's line, and thus it was fitting that he should be made like his brethren in all things" (Heb 2:14-17). And this likeness in all things has as a kind of beginning, or as the inception of the affair, his birth from a woman; his revelation in the flesh, even though in terms of his own nature he is invisible; his abasement in the human condition for the economy of salvation, even though he has the transcendent name; his humbling to manhood, even though he is raised high above the Thrones; and his acceptance of servile limitations, even though he is by nature the Lord (Phil 2:6f). And all this because "The Word was God" (Jn 1:1).

B. How right are your thoughts on this matter. Nonetheless you should know that in their opinion it is inadmissible and even unfitting either to think or to affirm that the Word who was ineffably and incomprehensibly born from God the Father had to undergo a second birth from a woman. They maintain that it was enough for him to have been born from the Father once only, in a manner fitting to God.

A. In that case they are finding fault with the Son, and saying that his decision to undergo a voluntary self-emptying for our sake was misguided. Surely in this way the great and venerable mystery of piety is frustrated and rendered futile, for are they not implying that the Only Begotten's wonderful economy in the flesh served no purpose for the inhabitants of earth? The word of truth does not allow the babblings of such people as this to gain the upper hand, on the contrary it shows them up for their most stupid ramblings wholly devoid of any knowledge of the mystery of Christ. God the Father engendered the Son from himself in one single act of generation, but it was his good pleasure to save the whole human race in him by means of the incarnation, or rather the enmanment, which, of course, evidently and entirely depended on birth from a woman; and for this end, that by the likeness that the Word born from God had with us, the law of sin in the members of our flesh could be condemned, and so that in the likeness of the death of the one who knew not death, death might be destroyed. As it is said: "If we have been conjoined with him in the likeness of his death, so also shall we be in the likeness of his resurrection" (Rom 6:5.). It follows, therefore, that He Who Is, The One Who Exists, is necessarily born of the flesh, taking all that is ours into himself so that all that is born of the flesh, that is us corruptible and perishing beings, might rest in him. In short, he took what was ours to be his very own so that we might have all that was his. "He was rich but he became poor for our sake, so that we might be enriched by his poverty" (2 Cor 8:9). When they say that the Word of God did not become flesh, or rather did not undergo birth from a woman according to the flesh, they bankrupt the economy of salvation, for if he who was rich did not impoverish himself, abasing himself to our condition out of tender love, then we have not gained his riches but are still in our poverty, still enslaved by sin and death, because the

Word becoming flesh is the undoing and the abolition of all that fell upon human nature as our curse and punishment. If they so pull up the root of our salvation, and dislodge the cornerstone of our hope, how will anything else be left standing? As I have said, if the Word has not become flesh then neither has the dominion of death been overthrown, and in no way has sin been abolished, and we are still held captive in the transgressions of the first man, Adam, deprived of any return to a better condition; a return which I would say has been gained by Christ the Savior of us all.

B. I understand what you are saying.

A. Then how should we define him who shares in flesh and blood along with us although in his own nature he is different from us? We would hardly say that it was fitting for any man to take a share in humanity, for how can one speak of something assuming a reality that is different from it if that reality was its own nature in the first place? Does my argument not make perfect sense?

B. Oh indeed so.

A. Look at it from another perspective. Is it not wicked and shocking to try to take away from God the Word his birth from a woman according to the flesh? For how could his body possibly give life to us if it were not the very own body of him who is Life? And how could it be that the "blood of Jesus cleanses us from all sin" (1 Jn 1:7) if it was in reality only that of an ordinary man subject to sin? And how has "God the Father sent his Son born of a woman, born subject to the law" (Gal 4:4)? Or how has "he condemned sin in the flesh" (Rom 8:3)? To condemn sin does not belong to someone with a nature like ours, under the tyranny of sin, an ordinary man. But insofar as it became the body of the one who knew no transgression, how rightly it could shake off the tyranny of sin to enjoy all the personal riches of the Word who is ineffably united with it in a manner beyond all description. Thus it is a holy and lifegiving thing, full of divine energy. And we too are transformed in Christ, the first-fruits, to be above corruption and sin. What the blessed Paul says is true: "Just as we bore the image of the earthly, so shall we bear the image of the heavenly" (1 Cor 15:49) that is to say, of Christ. Christ is understood as the Heavenly Man, not as if he brought down his flesh from on high and out of heaven, but because the Word who is God came down from out of heaven and entered our likeness, that is to say submitted to birth from a woman according to the flesh, while ever remaining what he was, that is one from on high, from heaven, superior to all things as God even with the flesh. This is what the divine John says about him somewhere: "He who comes from above is above all" (Jn 3:31). He remained Lord of all things even when he came, for the economy, in the form of a slave, and this is why the mystery of Christ is truly wonderful. Indeed God the Father said to the Jews through one of the prophets: "Look on this you scoffers, be struck with wonder and disappear, for I am doing a work in your days, a work in which you will not believe even if one were to explain it to you" (Hab 1:5, Acts 13:41). Indeed the mystery of Christ runs the risk of being disbelieved precisely because it is so incredibly wonderful. For God was in humanity. He who was above all creation was in our human condition; the invisible one was made visible in the flesh; he who is from the heavens and from on high was in the likeness of earthly things; the immaterial one could be touched; he who is free in his own nature came in the form of a slave; he who blesses all creation became accursed; he who is all righteousness was numbered among transgressors; life itself came in the appearance of death. All this followed because the body which tasted death belonged to no other but to him who is the Son by nature. Can you find fault in any of this, or in any of my other arguments?

B. None at all.

A. There are other things you ought to consider as well.

B. What do you mean?

A. Christ said somewhere to those who wanted to deny the resurrection of the dead: "Have you not read that he who made man in the beginning made them male and female?" (Mt 19:4), and the divine Paul also wrote: "Marriage and the undefiled bed is an entirely honorable thing" (Heb 13:4). In that case, when the Only Begotten Word of God wished to enter our likeness why did he not permit the laws of our human nature to apply in the constitution and generation of his own flesh? He did not commit himself to assume flesh through the marriage bed, but rather from a holy and unmarried virgin, conceiving from the Spirit when the power of God overshadowed her, as it is written. So if God did not hold marriage in dishonor, but on the contrary honored it with a blessing, then why did the Word, who is God, make a virgin the mother of his own flesh with a conception straight from the Holy Spirit?

B. I am unable to say.

A. Will the reason not become abundantly clear to anyone who reflects on it? As I have said, the Son came, or rather was made man, in order to reconstitute our condition within himself; first of all in his own holy, wonderful, and truly amazing birth and life. This was why he himself became the first one to be born of the Holy Spirit (I mean of course after the flesh) so that he could trace a path for grace to come to us. He wanted us to have this intellectual regeneration and spiritual assimilation to himself, who is the true and natural Son, so that we too might be able to call God our Father, and so remain free of corruption as no longer owning our first father, that is Adam, in whom we were corrupted. All this happened "not from blood, not from the will of the flesh, or the will of man" (Jn 1:13) but from God through the Spirit. Indeed Christ once said:

"Call no man on earth your father, for you have but one Father who is in heaven" (Mt 23:9). And because he came down into our condition solely in order to lead us to his own divine state, he also said: "I am going to my Father and your Father; to my God, and your God" (Jn 20:17). In his case the Heavenly One is his natural Father; in our case he is our God. But insofar as this true and natural Son became as we are, so he speaks of the Father as his God, a language fitting to his self-emptying. Still, he gave his very own Father even to us, for it is written: "Yet to those who did receive him, those that believed in his name, he gave them authority to become the children of God" (Jn 1:12). But if we foolishly deny that the Word of God the Father became like us by such a birth, the very one who has the dominion over all as the most wise Paul says (Col 1:18), then how else could we be so conformed as to be called the Children of God by the Spirit? Whom should we then take as the first-fruits of this process? Who, in short, would bring this dignity to us?

B. I am sure that even they would say that it was the Word made Man.

A. But how could that be the case unless he himself became flesh, that is became man, appropriating a human body to himself in such an indissoluble union that it has to be considered as his very own body and no one else's? This is how he transmits the grace of sonship even to us so that we too can become children of the Spirit, insofar as human nature had first achieved this possibility in him. It seems to me that the divine Paul was meditating on such thoughts when he so rightly wrote: "For just as we have borne the image of that which is earthly so shall we bear the image of the heavenly, for the first man was from the earth and earthly, but the second is from heaven." All those who belong to the earthly one bear the character of the earth, but all those who belong to the Heavenly One bear a

heavenly character (cf. 1 Cor 15:47-49). We are earthly beings
insofar as the curse of corruption has passed from the earthly
Adam even to us, and through our corruption the law of sin
entered in the members of our flesh. Yet we became heavenly
beings, receiving this gift in Christ. He is from God, from on
high, and naturally God, yet he came down to our condition in
a strange and most unusual manner, and was born of the Spirit,
according to the flesh, so that we too might abide in holiness
and incorruptibility like him. Clearly grace came upon us from
him, as from a new rootstock, a new beginning.

B. How excellently you put it.

A. So why is it said that "He was made like his brethren in
all things" (Heb 2:17), which means like us? How can we
possibly understand him as taking up our likeness unless he is
not of our condition, and different from us in nature? For
whatever is "made like" certain other things, must of necessity
be different from them, unlike them, indeed of a different form
or nature to them. The Only Begotten, therefore, was by nature
unlike us, and then he is said to have been made like us when
he became as we are, that is man. There was only one way,
however, that this could properly happen, and that was by a
human birth, even though in his case it happened so marvel-
ously since the one who became flesh was God. We must admit,
of course, that the body which he united to himself was endowed with a rational soul, for the Word, who is God, would
hardly neglect our finer part, the soul, and have regard only for
the earthly body. Quite clearly in all wisdom he provided for
both the soul and the body.

B. I agree. The way you think is right.

A. In that case, if our opponents insist that the holy virgin
must never be called Mother of God, but Mother of Christ
instead, then their blasphemy is patent, for they are denying
that Christ is really God and Son. If they really believed that he

was God, insofar as the Only Begotten came to be as we are, then why would they be afraid of calling her who gave him birth "the Mother of God"—I mean after the flesh?

B. Well, they say that the title of Christ is the only proper designation for the one who is born of a woman of David's race, since he was anointed by the Holy Spirit. But the Word of God needs no such anointing in his own nature, for by nature he is holy. Is it not true that the title Christ presupposes some kind of anointing has taken place?

A. You are right to conclude that he is called Christ only because of the anointing, just as an apostle is so called because of his apostolic function, and an angel from his office as messenger. Names like these clearly indicate certain functions rather than individual realities or specific persons. Even the prophets are called Christs, as it is sung in the Psalms: "Do not touch my Christs, and do no harm against my prophets" (Ps 105:15) The prophet Habbakuk also said: "You came forth for the salvation of your people, to save your Christs" (Hab 3:13). But tell me this; is it not true that even they would admit that there is only one Christ and Son, who is the Lord made man, the Only Begotten of God made flesh?

B. They might admit this but really they do not want the title Christ applied to the Word born of God the Father, since in his own nature, as God, he was never anointed. They would also maintain that this too is one of those names which we cannot use about the Holy Spirit or the Father himself.

A. The logic behind this is not very clear. It would be a good thing if you could explain it.

B. Well, listen. There are many varied titles which the inspired scriptures apply to the Son. He is called: God, Lord, Light, and Life, as well as King, Lord of Hosts, Holy One, and Lord of All. If someone wished to apply all these titles to the Father himself, or to the Holy Spirit, he could do so without error. This is because in a single nature there can only be one excellence of dignities. They argue from this that if the title Christ is truly appropriate to the Only Begotten, then it should be, like the other titles, equally applicable without distinction to the Father himself and to the Holy Spirit. Given that it is entirely inappropriate to apply this title to the Father or to the Holy Spirit, then neither can it be right to apply it to the Only Begotten, and on the contrary, they say, it ought in fact to be attributed to the one who is of the line of David, for in our arguments and discourses we can quite properly attribute to him an anointing by the Holy Spirit.

A. We ourselves also admit that the titles of the divine perfections are common to the Father, the Son, and the Holy Spirit, and we crown the Begetter with equal glories to the One Begotten from him, and the Holy Spirit too. Nonetheless, dear friends, I would say that that the title Christ, and that which it signifies (that is, an anointing) really do apply to the Only Begotten, after the manner of his self-emptying. It indicates quite clearly to those who hear it that he has undergone an incarnation, for it signifies wonderfully well that he has been anointed in being made man. If we were not considering this issue of the economy in the flesh, but rather were to direct our thoughts to the Only Begotten Word of God considered outside all the limitations of the self-emptying, then yes, it would indeed be entirely unfitting to name him Christ when he has not been anointed. Since the divine and sacred scripture says that he has become flesh, however, even the anointing is appropriate for him, referring to the incarnation which is his own. The all-wise Paul puts it this way: "For the Sanctifier and the sanctified all have the same origin. This is why he is not ashamed to call them brothers when he says: I will announce your name to my brethren" (Heb 2:11-12; Ps 44:7-8). He was sanctified along with us when he became like us. The divine

David also testifies that the one who is truly Son was also anointed in accordance with his becoming flesh, which is to say perfect man, when he addresses these words to him: "Your throne O God is from age to age; a scepter of righteousness is the scepter of your kingdom. You have loved righteousness and hated wickedness, and so God, your God, has anointed you with the oil of gladness above all who participate in you" (Ps 45:6-7 LXX).[3] Take note, then, that while David calls him God and attributes to him an eternal throne, he also says that he has been anointed by God, evidently the Father, with a special anointing above that of his participants, which means us. The Word who is God has become man, therefore, but has retained all the while the virtues of his proper nature. He is perfection itself, and as John says: "full of grace and truth" (Jn 1:14), and while he himself has everything that is fitting to the deity, we on our part "have all of us received from his fullness" as it is written (Jn 1:16). Nonetheless he made the limits of the manhood his own, and all the things that pertain to it, and for this reason he is called Christ even though he cannot be thought of as anointed when we consider him specifically as God or when we speak about his divine nature. How else could we consider that there is one Christ, One Son and Lord, if the Only Begotten had disdained the anointing and had never come under the limitations of the self-emptying?

B. But they move along completely different lines to us, and interpret the holy mystery foolishly. They maintain that God the Word assumed a perfect man who was of the line of Abraham and David, as the scriptures say, and who was of the same nature as his ancestors, a man complete in his nature, composed of a rational soul and human flesh. They say that this man, of our nature, was fashioned by the power of the Holy

3 Cyril applies the Septuagint version to distinguish Christ (who has the glory of God by nature—*kata physin*) from all others, such as prophets.

Spirit in the womb of the virgin and "was born of a woman, born under the law, so that he could redeem us all" (Gal 4:4-5.) from the law's slavery as we received the sonship long destined for us. They say that God the Word conjoined this man to himself in an entirely new way, bringing him to death as is the law among men, but raising him from the dead and taking him up to heaven and sitting him at the right hand of God so that he was "above every Principality and Authority, every Power and Dominion, and every name that can be named, not only in this age but even in the age to come" (Eph 1:21). They say that he received the worship of all the creation insofar as he had an inseparable conjunction with the divine nature, as all creation rendered its worship to him with intellectual reference to God.[4] It is for this reason that one does not speak of two Sons or two Lords because God the Word, the Only Begotten Son of the Father, is the Son by nature, and this man is connected with him and participates in him and thereby shares in the very title and honor of the Son. The Lord, who by nature is God the Word, communicates the honor to this man who is conjoined with him, and this is why we do not speak of two Sons or two Lords since it is obvious that he who is Lord and Son by nature has, for the sake of salvation, assumed a man into an inseparable conjunction with himself which thereby elevates him to the title and honor of both Son and Lord.

A. My goodness. I cannot imagine how stupid and intellectually superficial they must be who hold to such a conception. The whole thing is faithlessness and nothing else. It is the novelty of wicked inventions, the overthrowing of the divine and sacred kerygma which has proclaimed One Lord Jesus Christ, the Son of God, truly the Word of God the Father who was made man and incarnated so that the same one is equally God and man, and that to him alone apply all the divine and

4 Jesus as notionally being honored with the divine titles.

human characteristics. For he who is and exists from all eternity, as he is God, underwent birth from a woman according to the flesh. This means that it pertains to one and the same both to exist and subsist eternally, and also to have been born after the flesh in these last times. He who as God was holy by nature has been sanctified along with us in terms of his manifestation as man, for it befits man to be sanctified. Both he who exists in lordly glories, and he who took the form of a slave as his own, calls God his Father. He who as God is Life and Life-Giver is said to have been brought to life by the Father in terms of his manifestation as man. This is why all these characteristics pertain to him. He did not disdain the economy which even God the Father had praised, if what Paul taught is true, who said somewhere, "He made him who knew not sin into sin for our sake so that in him we might become the righteousness of God" (2 Cor 5:21); and in another place, "He did not spare his own Son but gave him up for the sake of all so that with him he might grant us all things" (Rom 8:32). Surely our exposition follows the mind of the scriptures?

B. Most certainly.

A. Our opponents have chosen to hold and teach that the Only Begotten Word of God assumed a man of the line of the divine David and Abraham, and took care to form him in the holy virgin, then conjoined himself to him, made him come to the trial of death, raised him from the dead, took him up to heaven, and seated him at the right hand of God. But if this is the case then it seems to me that the holy Fathers and all the God-inspired scriptures, and we ourselves, are speaking in vain when we say that he became man. Nonetheless I think that it is exactly this, and nothing else, that the all-wise John meant when he wrote: "The Word became flesh" (Jn 1:14). It seems to me that they have turned the mystery of the economy in the flesh completely on its head, for in their argument one cannot see how God the Word, born of God, and God by nature, abased himself to a self-emptying and humbled himself to assume the form of a slave. On the contrary, in their estimate a man is exalted into the glory of the Godhead and into preeminence over all things; he receives the form of God and is raised on high and comes to be enthroned alongside the Father. Or do I not speak the truth?

B. Oh yes, entirely so.

A. But if their argument is true, that the Only Begotten disdained the economy, what was so shameful in it that caused him to despise it (Heb 12:2)? And how was he able to become "obedient to the Father even unto death, death on a cross" (Phil 2:8)? And if it was true that he assumed a man, brought him to the trial of death, raised him to the heavens and made him sit alongside the Father, then where would the Only Begotten position his own throne after this? For it is part of their argument that there are not two Sons, only one enthroned with God, and he seems clearly to be the one who is of the line of David and Abraham. But if this were so, how could the Only Begotten be said to have been the Savior of the World? Would he not rather have been the Patron and Promoter of that man by whom we were saved? In such a case the fulfilment of the law and the prophets would then turn out to be a man, someone different than him, because the law speaks of the mystery of Christ, and Moses wrote about him and became our pedagogue in relation to him (Gal 3:24). I fear that the faith has come to nothing, leaked away, so that our whole venerable mystery is made entirely void. The excellent Paul has already clearly announced this when he said: "Do not say in your heart, Who shall rise up to heaven so as to bring Christ down? or Who shall descend to the abyss so as to bring Christ back up? For what does scripture say? The Word is near you, in your mouth and in your heart. It is the word of faith which I preach; for if you confess with your mouth that Jesus is Lord, and believe in your heart that God raised him from the dead, then you will be saved" (Rom 10:6-9). If we are to believe what these perverted people say about a man assumed and united to God the Word by a relationship, that he died and came back to life, and was exalted to heaven, then how is the mystery of religion any longer great or admirable or extraordinarily wonderful? It is past all belief that such a man, who is not God truly or by nature, should parade himself in a divine situation (doubtless having ousted him who is the Son by nature) and that the angels and archangels, or even the Seraphim who are higher still, should stand before him ready to do service for someone who is not truly Son or God, but in reality is a man who has received the title of sonship, and divine honors in the form of great benefits in which he participates just as is the case with us. Our opponents come out with such things as these without the slightest sense of shame. Surely their teaching represents the ultimate in sacrilege and impiety? For anything that is given or bestowed can be rejected, and it is obvious that anything that is externally introduced can be lost. I will pass over the other blasphemies and nonsense in their arguments, but why do they drag down the most wonderful part of the economy to a disgraceful level and make out our most holy worship as nothing more than the idolatry of a man? They steal the worship from him who is really the Son, and persuade us to worship someone conjoined to him in some kind of relationship instead, someone (so they say) who has risen over every Principality and Authority and Dominion. In this way they have implicated not only everyone on earth, but even the rational heavenly powers too in the guilt of a deception, if they, like us, are found to be worshipping not the true and natural Son made man, the Word who shone forth from God the Father's very being, but rather some other person apart from him, a man of the line of David, a man who has only been given the external appearances of deity by God's will as if they were external decorations, but someone who is not God in truth.

B. They would say that even though he might be personally understood to be a man, nonetheless he receives divine worship from the whole creation in terms of an intellectual reference to God.

A. But tell me please how we can understand or articulate this business of "reference" which they are always going on about? Come, let us investigate the divine and sacred scripture and let us seek the solution there. Well the Israelites had little reverence for God and bitterly attacked Moses and Aaron, so Moses addressed them: "Who is Aaron that you murmur against him? Your murmuring is not against us but against God" (Num 16:11; Ex 16:8). They had ostensibly offended Moses and Aaron, but what they had done touched the divine glory, and the deeper motive of the traducers "had reference" to this glory. Moses and Aaron, however, were not gods, nor did the Creation ever worship them "in reference" to God. God ruled over the fleshly Israel through the prophets. Then they came to the divine Samuel and said: "Make us a King like the rest of the nations" (1 Sam 8:5). When he heard this the Spirit-bearer was grieved, and rightly so, but he heard God speaking: "It is not you they have rejected but me, that I should no longer rule over them" (1 Sam 8:7). Here we see again, quite clearly, that this rejection has God as its reference. Even the Lord and Savior of all says this about the wretched: "Whatever you do to one of the least of these, you do to me" (Mt 25:40). Are we to conclude that if someone worships the one who is of the line of David, he can be said to have worshipped the Son? And if someone refuses to believe in such a son are we to think he has really offended the natural Son whose only desire is that we should honor and believe in this man in just the same way and degree that we do him? If this were to be the case would not the slave have been held in the same honor as the Lord since he is elevated to the eminence of the deity? But in that case "God is increased" as the scriptures say (Ps 81:10 LXX), and surely something of an unequal nature must have been added to the holy and consubstantial Trinity, so as to receive worship along with it, and share in the same glory?

B. They would say that this "reference" ought to be taken in some sense like this: that insofar as we understand that the Word of God is inseparably conjoined to the descendant of David, so we worship him as God.

A. But is this mere conjunction with the Word enough to allow him to grasp the proper glory of God and rise above the bounds of the created order? Does this make him an object of worship even though he is not God? I notice, for example, how someone in the Psalms sings this to God: "My soul is bound to you" (Ps 63:8), and the blessed Paul also writes: "Whoever is bound to the Lord is one spirit with him" (1 Cor 6:17). So tell me, should we also worship such people as this, since they too have a bonding "in reference" to God? But even so, the term "bonding" surely has a stronger and much more suitable significance than to speak of a "conjunction," for does not someone with a bonding experience an extreme form of conjunction?

B. So it would seem.

A. Then why do they abandon the term "union," even though it is the word in customary use among us, and indeed has come down to us from the holy Fathers, preferring to call it a conjunction? The term union in no way causes the confusion of the things it refers to, but rather signifies the concurrence in one reality of those things which are understood to be united. Surely it is not only those things which are simple and homogeneous which hold a monopoly over the term "unity"? for it can also apply to things compounded out of two, or several, or different kinds of things. This is the considered opinion of the experts in such matters. How wicked they are, then, when they divide in two the one true and natural Son incarnated and made man, and when they reject the union and call it a conjunction, something that any other man could have with God, being bonded to him as it were in terms of virtue and holiness. One of the prophets rightly spoke of this in relation to those who had fallen into negligence: "Be gathered again and tied back together, you undisciplined nation, before you become like a flower that passes away" (Zeph 2:1-2 LXX). A disciple can also be said to "attach" himself to a teacher in terms of a love of study, and we too can attach ourselves to one another not in one fashion only but in many. In short, when someone assists another in a task, should we not consider that he has been conjoined by will to the one who receives his assistance? It seems to us that this is exactly what these innovators mean by conjunction. You must have heard how they stupidly maintain that God the word assumed a man, as if he were a different son to himself, and then proposed him as a kind of assistant to his designs so that he underwent the trial of death, came to life again, rose up to heaven, and even sat upon the throne of the ineffable Godhead? With arguments such as these have they not completely and utterly proven that this man is altogether different from the true and natural son?

B. I would say so.

A. But once they have slipped down to this level of stupidity, as to think and say that the Only Begotten Word of God did not himself become as we are, but rather assumed a man, then in what way do they want us to understand the terms of such an assumption? Would it be as if he had foreordained that someone should accomplish a desired task, in the way that one of the prophets talks about: "I was no prophet, or son of a prophet. I was a goatherd and dresser of sycamores, and the Lord took me from among the flock, and the Lord said to me: Go prophesy to my people Israel" (Am 7:14-15). From being a goatherd, God made him into a prophet and appointed him as an assistant in his own designs.

B. They too would say that the "assumption" was certainly not of this order, but that we should understand it in terms of the "taking the form of a slave" (Phil 2:7).

A. In that case it would seem to be the proper conclusion that the one assumed in this inseparable union has become the personal property of the one assuming, and while Jesus is God, the one and only true Son of God, the Word of God the Father born of God before all ages and times, nonetheless the same one, in these last times of the present age, has been born of a woman according to the flesh, for the form of a slave belongs to no other, but was his very own.

B. What do you mean?

A. Well, tell me this: what is the proper referent for the phrase "taking the form of a slave"? Is it something which was already a slave by nature, or something which was truly free and naturally above the limits of slavery?

B. I would suppose it was something which was free; for how could anything start to be what it already was by nature?

A. In that case take note that the Only Begotten Word of God, even though he had become as we are and had come under the limitations of slavery, in accordance with his human nature, still bore witness to the fact he was naturally free when he jointly paid the drachmas and said: "And so the sons are free" (Mt 17:26). Does it not follow that he receives the form of a slave and appropriates the characteristics of this self-emptying, and does not disdain this likeness to us? For there was no other way to honor the slave except by making the characteristics of the slave his very own so that they could be illumined from his own glory. What is pre-eminent will always conquer, and the shame of the slavery is thus borne away from us. He who was above us became as we are, and he who is naturally free was in the limitations of our life. This was why honors passed even to us, for we too are called the sons of God, and we regard his own true Father as our Father also. All that is human has become his own. And so, to say that he assumed the form of a slave expresses the whole mystery of the economy in the flesh. So, if they confess One Lord and Son, the Word of God the Father, but say that a simple man of the line of David was conjoined as a companion of his sonship and his glory, then it is time for us to speak to people who choose to think like this with sorrowful compassion. We will say: "Who shall give water for my head, and a spring of tears for my eyes, that I might weep for this people day and night?" (Jer 8:23) for they have veered to an evil opinion and "denied the Lord who redeemed them" (2 Pet 2:1; Rom 1:28). It seems to us that there are two sons in this argument, who are unequal in nature, and that a slave is crowned with the glory that is proper to God, and that some bastard son is decked out with the selfsame dignities as the one who is really God's natural Son, even though God says quite clearly: "I will not give my glory to another" (Is 42:8). How can someone who has only been honored with a mere conjunction fail to be "other" to the true and natural Son when he has just been assumed for the office of servant, given the honor of sonship, just like us, and sharing in another's glory which he attains by grace and favor?

B. So the Emmanuel must not be separated out into a man, considered as distinct from God the Word?

A. On no account. I say that we must call him God made man, and that both the one and the other are this same reality, for he did not cease to be God when he became man, nor did he regard the economy as unacceptable by disdaining the limitations involved in the self-emptying.

B. They would argue that if this were the case then his body must be consubstantial with the Word. For only in this way, and no other, could he be regarded as one single Son.

A. What nonsense that is. Surely it is the clearest proof of a delirious brain. How could one posit an identity of essence in things which are so disparate in the rationale of their respective natures? Godhead is one thing, manhood quite another. So, what are these things which we say have come into unification? One cannot speak of things "united" when there is only one thing to start with; there must be two or more.

B. This is why they argue that these things we name are separate realities.

A. But they are not separated, as I have already said, in terms of individual distinctnesses, so that they exist apart and distant from one another. On the contrary they are brought together into an indissoluble union, for, as John says: "The Word became flesh" (Jn 1:14).

B. In that case both natures must have been confused, and have become one.

A. But who would be so misguided and stupid as to think that the divine nature of the Word had changed into something which formerly it was not? or that the flesh was changed by some kind of transformation into the nature of the Word himself? This is impossible. We say that there is one Son, and that he has one nature even when he is considered as having assumed flesh endowed with a rational soul. As I have already said, he has made the human element his own. And this is the way, not otherwise, that we must consider that the same one is at once God and man.

B. Then he does not have two natures? that of God, and that of man?

A. Well, Godhead is one thing, and manhood is another thing, considered in the perspective of their respective and intrinsic beings, but in the case of Christ they came together in a mysterious and incomprehensible union without confusion or change. The manner of this union is entirely beyond conception.

B. But how from these two things, that is Godhead and manhood, can we envisage a single Christ?

A. I think in no other way than as things which come together with each other in an indivisible union beyond all conception, as I have already said.

B. Such as what?

A. Well, do we not say that a human being like ourselves is one, and has a single nature, even though he is not homogeneous but really composed of two things, I mean soul and body?

B. We do.

A. And if someone takes the flesh on its own, separating its unity with its own soul, and divides what was one into two, have they not destroyed the proper conception of a man?

B. And yet the all-wise Paul writes: "For if our outer man is being destroyed, nevertheless the inner man is being renewed day by day" (2 Cor 4:16).

A. You speak rightly for he knew, and knew perfectly well, what were the constituents of the one man, and he makes a distinction between them as only theoretically conceivable. He calls the soul the inner man, and the flesh the outer man. I am reminded of the holy scriptures where we sometimes find the whole living being signified in terms of a part, as when God says: "I will pour out my Spirit on all flesh" (Jl 2:28), and again when Moses addresses the Israelites: As seventy five souls did your fathers go down into Egypt" (Dt 10:22). We will find that the same thing has happened with regard to Emmanuel himself. After the union (I mean with the flesh) even if anyone calls him Only Begotten, or God from God, this does not mean he is thought of as being separated from the flesh or indeed the manhood. Similarly if one calls him a man, this is not to take away the fact that he is God and Lord.

B. But if we say that the Son (even considering him as incarnate) has a single nature, surely it is completely inevitable that we must admit a confusion and a mixture here, as if he had hidden away a human nature in himself. For what would the nature of man be in the face of the pre-eminence of the godhead?

A. My friend, if anyone says that when we speak of the single nature of God the Word incarnate and made man we imply that a confusion or mixture has occurred, then they are talking utter rubbish. No one could convict us of saying this by the force of proper arguments. But if they intend to impose their own preferences on us, like a law, then "they have devised a plan which they cannot secure" (Ps 21:11) for we must pay heed to the God-inspired scripture rather than to them. If they think that because the nature of man is as nothing before the divine pre-eminence, then this means that it must be "hidden away" and overwhelmed, as they keep saying, then once more we reply: "You are mistaken, for you know neither the scriptures nor the power of God" (Mt 22:29). It was not impossible to God, in his loving-kindness, to make himself capable of bearing the limitations of the manhood. And he foretold this to us in enigmas when he initiated Moses, depicting the manner of the incarnation in types. For he came down in the form of fire onto the bush in the desert, and the fire played upon the shrub but did not consume it. When he saw this Moses was amazed. Why was there no compatibility here between the wood and the fire? How did this inflammable substance endure the assaults of the flame? Well, as I have already said, this event was a type of a mystery, of how the divine nature of the Word supported the limitations of the manhood; because he chose to. Absolutely nothing is impossible to him (Mk 10:27).

B. As well you know, they refuse to think of the matter like this.

A. Doubtless we will find their way of thinking to be offering us two sons and two Christs?

B. No, not two. They say that the Word of God the Father, who is Son by nature, is one; but that the man who is assumed is by nature the Son of David, and is the Son of God insofar as he is assumed by God the Word. They say that he has come to such dignity and has the sonship by grace, because God the Word dwells within him.

A. What has happened to their brains and their intelligence—people who hold such opinions? How can they possibly say there is not a duality of sons when they split off man and God from each other? If, as they say, one is truly the Son by nature, but the other has the sonship by grace and came to such dignity because of the Word dwelling within him, then what more does he have than us? For the Word also dwells in us. The most holy Paul confirms this point for us when he says: "For this reason I bend my knees before the Father, from whom all fatherhood is named in heaven and on earth. May he grant that you are strengthened in power through his Spirit, according to the riches of his glory, that Christ may dwell in your hearts" (Eph 3:14-17); and he is within us by the Spirit, "in whom we cry out Abba, Father" (Rom 8:15). And so, if we have been granted the same dignity by God the Father, our position is in no way inferior to his. For we too are sons and gods by grace, and we have surely been brought to this wonderful and supernatural dignity since we have the Only Begotten Word of God dwelling within us. It is completely wicked and foolish for them to say that Jesus has been granted the dignity of the Sonship and has won this glory as a matter of grace.

B. Will you explain why?

A. Indeed I will. In the first place, as I said earlier, this implies that he must be considered as a different and separate Son and Christ and Lord from the one who is truly and naturally such. And secondly, another impossible consequence is introduced which obviously flies in the face of right reason.

B. Will you say what it is?

A. The all-wise John said about Christ: "He came to what was his own and his own did not receive him, but as many as did receive him he gave them the authority to become the children of God" (Jn 1:11-12). Well then, if he has the sonship by grace and has come to be what he is by winning this extra dignity will he be led to grant to others the riches it cost him so much to gain himself? Do you not think that the whole scheme is highly unlikely?

B. Most certainly so.

A. When something does not arise from a nature, but instead is added on from outside, is there not always the possibility of losing it?

B. How could it be otherwise?

A. In that case it will be a possible eventuality for the Son one day to fall from his sonship, since whatever is not stabilized by natural laws is not totally assured against loss.

B. This is true.

A. We can see from another point of view how ill-conceived their doctrine is, and how it really proceeds from the worst kind of evil intent. If it is true that whatever is by adoption or grace must always be in the likeness of that which is by nature and truth, then how can we be sons by adoption in reference to him who is truly the Son, if even he stands alongside us in the number of those who have the sonship by grace? How is it in the Gospel parable that he is sent as the Son after the servants? And when they see him the vineyard tenants say: "This is the heir; come let us kill him" (Mt 21:38)? The one who appeared in the flesh, therefore, and suffered the wickedness of the Jews, is truly the Son, and is free, since he is born of a nature that is free. Insofar as we consider him as God he is not in the ranks of those who are under the yoke, and even though he became a son under the yoke of slavery, just like us, still, as I have said, he is truly the Son by nature who is beyond any yoke, and above all creation. It is in relation to him that we too have been fashioned as sons by adoption and grace.

B. But they argue that we do not talk about the man as being the son of God by nature and that this avoids talking of two sons. Just as the Word, who comes down from heaven, is not by nature the Son of David, so too he who is of the line of David is not Son of God by nature.

A. But in this case they have split him into two sons, and both of them are proven to claim the title falsely. I think one might conclude that if things are really as our opponents foolishly maintain, then the mystery of Christ is a useless posture. Where would be the union? and what was the point of it? Perhaps even the fact that the Word became flesh is shown up now as a falsity or a superfluous extra, if the Word of God the Father is not to be called Son of David insofar as he became his descendant according to the flesh? But I think we need to tell them what Christ himself said to the Jewish teachers: "What do you think of Christ? Whose son is he?" (Mt 22:42). And if they should answer, "David's son," then we will tell them: "How then did David, in the Spirit, call him Lord, when he said: The Lord said to my Lord, Sit at my right hand while I make your enemies a footstool for your feet? If David, therefore, in the Spirit, calls him Lord, then how can he be his son?" (Mt 22:43-45). Tell me, does one who is not truly and naturally the Son sit alongside God on the same throne as him who rules over all things? This is what our opponents are saying. But, as the all-wise Paul says, the Father "has never said to any of the angels: You are my Son (Heb 1:5), nor has he said: Sit on my right" (Heb 1:13). How, then, can a man born of a woman be in these supreme honors, on the very throne of the godhead, and "above every Principality, Dominion, Throne, and Authority, and every name that can be named" (Eph 1:21)? Notice how the Lord says: "If David, therefore, in the Spirit, calls him Lord, then how can he be his son?" This persuades all who want to search out the truth to maintain that the Word, even when he came to participate in flesh and blood, has even so remained one Son. He bears witness that he is God from a divine pre-eminence and dominion, and how well he indicates that he has become man by also being called the Son of David.

B. I would suppose that they will reply to this: "But are we, then, to admit that he who is of the very being of God the Father is exactly the same as he who is of the line of David?

A. Well that is a stupid question is it not? unworthy of the power of the mystery and unworthy of anyone who delights in the truth.

B. Explain why.

A. You must not divide him who is of David's line by saying that he is someone different to the one Christ and Son and Lord, for the correct position is that the Only Begotten Son who is born from God the Father is himself, and no other, the Son of David according to the flesh. They must not maintain, therefore, in a boundless folly, that just as the Word of God who came down from heaven is not by nature David's son, so too he who is of David's line is not the Son of God by nature. As I said earlier, when the Word of God, who in nature and truth shone forth from God the Father, had assumed flesh and blood, he remained the same, that is truly and naturally the Son of the Father. He is the one and only Son, not one son alongside another son, considered in this way to be one person (*prosopon*). In this way we can gather into a true unity, though one that transcends speech and understanding, realities which were unlike one another, and separated because of their respective natures. This is how we can make progress along the infallible path of faith. For we say that the one and the same Jesus Christ is from God the Father as God the Word, and also of the line of godly David according to the flesh. Or do you think that I have not considered these matters correctly?

B. Oh, entirely so.

A. But I have another question for our opponents.

B. And what is it?

A. Do they not take it as axiomatic that the Only Begotten Word of God has his being from God the Father while, on their own admission, they maintain that the man who is assumed into a conjunction is born of the line of the divine David?

B. This is what they say.

A. Then the Word, being God, will surely surpass in every conceivable way, in nature and in glory, the man who is of David's line, and will have the advantage over him to the same extent that there is a difference in their natures. But, if I am right in what I say, why do they make a distinction and present one who bestows the glory and authority and the other who receives it so as to gain what he is as a gift or as a reward? The one who receives is surely inferior and subordinate to the one who gives, and the same applies when one glorifies and the other participates in the glory that comes from him.

B. I think that they too would admit the vast difference between God and man.

A. Then how is it that the all-wise Paul, the priest of the divine mysteries, who had indwelling within him the one of whom he preached, when he speaks in the Spirit calls by the name of God the very one who is of the Jews according to the flesh, and says that he is "blessed for all ages, Amen." What is there that is above "God who is over all" (cf. Rom 9:5)? What can we discern that is greater in God the Word born of the Father than the one born of the Jews according to the flesh, if he is different from him, and not properly and really the Son?

B. But they would say that he who is of David's line was

admitted by a conjunction, and seeing that God the Word dwelt within him he shared in his dignities and honors. The most holy Paul teaches this when he says about him: "He became obedient to the Father even to death, death on a cross. So God has highly exalted him and granted him the name above every name" (Phil 2:5-9), and this name is God.

A. Do they maintain that God has given "the name above every name" separately to the Son of David as if to a different son altogether?

B. Yes, this is what they say. For how could the Only Begotten, who is from God by nature, ever be given what he already possesses?

A. In that case, if this gift does not apply to him we must examine very carefully what the divine Paul himself has written about him: "Let each of you have that same mind which was in Christ Jesus, who even though he was in the form of God did not count equality with God a thing to be grasped, but emptied himself, assuming the form of a slave, coming in the likeness of men and being found in fashion as a man he humbled himself becoming obedient to death, death on a cross. And so, God highly exalted him and granted him the name above every name" (Phil 2:5-9). So if they maintain that it is the one who is of David's line, the man considered separately on his own, who has received the name above every name, then let them demonstrate how he pre-existed in the form of God and did not count equality with God a thing to be grasped, and how he assumed the form of a slave, evidently as though he did not already have it and did not exist in this way before he assumed it, even though (as they themselves prefer to say and think) he himself was the form of the slave. But if this were so how could he have assumed that form as if he did not already have it? Or how could this man be understood as "coming in the likeness of men"? and "being found in fashion as a man"? The very force of the arguments must surely bring them round, however unwilling they might be, to know the truth.

B. Which is?

A. That it is none other than God the Word, who exists in the form of God the Father, the impress of his very being (Heb 1:3), who is equal in all things to the one who begot him, who has emptied himself out. And what is this "emptying out"? It is his life in the form of a slave, in the flesh which he assumes; it is the likeness to us of one who is not as we are in his own nature, since he is above all creation. In this way he humbled himself, economically submitting himself to the limitations of the manhood. But even so he was God, for he did not have as a gift what pertained to him by nature. This was why he also said to God the Father who is in heaven: "Father, glorify me with that glory I had with you before the world was" (Jn 17:5). I do not think that they would say that it was David's descendant, born in the last times of this age, who was reclaiming as his own a glory that predated the world, at least if he is a different son and distinct from the true and natural Son? No, surely this is a saying which befits the godhead? It was necessary, yes necessary, that he should be conformed to us in the limitations of the manhood while at the same time he authentically enjoyed transcendent divine status within his own essential being; just as it is with the Father. How can the saying be true: "You must not introduce another god among you" (Ps 81:9), if according to them a man is deified by a conjunction with the Word and is said to be enthroned with God so as to share the Father's dignity?

B. How right you are.

A. And how can we correctly understand what is so wisely said in that text of Paul's: "For even if there are many gods and many lords in heaven and on earth, yet for us there is One God, the Father from whom are all things; and we too are through him" (1 Cor 8:5-6). And since there is One Lord Jesus Christ, through whom all things have been brought into being, as has been said so well, what shall we do, my friends, when you make a distinction between the Word of God the Father and the "assumed man," as you call him? Which one of these shall we say was the creator of the universe?

B. Surely it was the natural Son of God the Father, that is the Only Begotten?

A. But our priest of the divine mysteries tells us that all things have come into existence through Jesus Christ, and that this same Jesus is one and single. I remember that when we investigated the title "Christ" we said that it introduced the notion of anointing, for someone is called a Christ on account of having been anointed. So either let them confess that the Word of God the Father has been anointed in his own nature, and thus stood in need of the communion and sanctification of the Spirit, or let them teach us how someone who has never been anointed can be understood as Christ, or how the Only Begotten Word of God can be independently called Jesus, as when the blessed Gabriel said to the holy virgin: "Do not be afraid Mary, for behold, you shall conceive in your womb and bear a son, and you shall name him Jesus, for he shall save his people from their sins" (Lk 1:30-31; Mt 1:21).

B. Are we to say, then, that all things were made through a man, and that he who undergoes this birth from a woman in these last times of this age is the Creator of heaven and earth, the sum of all that they contain?

A. Well then, you tell me the answers to these questions: Did the Word not become flesh? Has he not been called The Son of Man? Did he not assume the form of a slave? Did he not empty himself, coming in the likeness of men and being found in fashion as a man? If they deny the economy, therefore, the divine disciples will stand against them saying: "And we saw, and we bear witness that the Father has sent his Son as Savior of the world, and whoever confesses that Jesus is the Son of God, then God abides in him and he in God" (1 Jn 4:14-15). And again: "The Spirit of God is made known in this, that every spirit which confesses that Jesus Christ has come in the flesh, is of God, and every spirit which does not confess Jesus, is not of God" (1 Jn 4:2-3). Besides, what sense does it make to think of a man as "coming in the flesh"? To come in the flesh and thereby to come into the world while always remaining what he was, applies rather to someone who is outside flesh, and who is not of our nature. And so, even if he did become man, there is nothing in this to hinder us from understanding that all things come into being through him, insofar as he is considered as God, and coeternal with the Father. God the Word did not change even when he assumed flesh endowed with a rational soul. This does not mean that he connected a man to himself as these innovators of the faith say, but that he himself became flesh, as I said, that is became man. In this way the anointing applies to him and is free from all objection. He is called Jesus because it is he himself who truly undergoes birth from a woman according to the flesh. In this way he saved his own people, not as a man conjoined to God, but as God who has come in the likeness of those who were in danger, so that in him first of all the human race might be refashioned to what it was in the beginning. In him all things became new (cf. 2 Cor 5:17).

B. In that case we must refuse to think or say that a man has been conjoined to God the Word so as to have fellowship in his dignity and enjoy the sonship in the order of grace; is that right?

A. Entirely so. The mind of the holy scriptures does not admit anything like this. It is rather an invention of a weak and feeble spirit that loves novelty and has no perception of the depth of the mystery. Where do the divine scriptures speak of

anything like this? On the contrary, the divine Paul clearly and
brilliantly describes the mystery of the incarnation of the Only
Begotten when he says: "Since the children share the same flesh
and blood, he too equally shared in these things so that by his
death he might bring to nothing him who had the power of
death, that is the devil" (Heb 2:14). And in another place he
does the same when he says: "For God sent his own Son in the
likeness of sinful flesh for the sake of sin so that he might judge
sin in the flesh, something the law could not do because it was
weakened by the flesh; and he did this to fulfil the righteousness
of the law among us who walk no longer according to the flesh
but according to the spirit" (Rom 8:3-4). We follow the mind
of the divinely inspired writers, and for this reason we say that
the one who participated in flesh and blood is not one who had
flesh and blood as his proper nature, and could not be otherwise,
but rather one who did not have this kind of existence but was
of a different nature to us. We say, therefore, that he came forth
from a woman, and in the likeness of sinful flesh, he who for
our sake became as we are, and yet is above us insofar as he is
understood as God. The Word became flesh, but not sinful
flesh, rather "in the likeness of sinful flesh." He lived as a man
with earthly beings, and came in our likeness, but he was not
subject to sin like us, but was far beyond the knowledge of any
transgression. The same one was at once God and man. I cannot
understand how these people, who pillage this wonderful and
noble economy of the Only Begotten, connect a man to him in
terms of a relationship adorned with external honors and radiant
in a glory which is not his, for then he is not truly God but
someone who has fellowship and participation with God, and
is thus a falsely-named son, a saved savior, a redeemed re-
deemer; all of which contradicts what the blessed Paul wrote:
"For the grace of God which is the salvation of all men has been
revealed so that, renouncing unrighteousness and worldly de-

sires, we might live soberly and religiously in the present age, waiting for the blessed hope and revelation of the glory of our great God and Savior Jesus Christ" (Tit 2:11-13).

B. But they would agree, saying that since he was judged entirely worthy of the conjunction with God the Word, he was called Great God even though he came from the line of David.

A. My goodness! What madness this is. As it is written: "flattering themselves they are wise, they have become as fools" (Rom 1:22). As I have said, they have changed the significance of the mystery of Christ round to its complete negation, for to say that he has been judged worthy is nothing else than to call him common man, and foolishly to divide him into complete diversity such that we must consider there are two sons to worship, where one is the true and natural son, but the other is an adopted, bastard son having nothing of his own. It can be said of him just as well as of us: "What then do you have which you have not received?" (1 Cor 4:7). What was it the all-wise Paul meant when he said: "For Jesus Christ, the Son of God, whom Silvanus, Timothy and myself preached among you, was not Yes and No; there was only Yes in him" (2 Cor 1:19). If one says that he was God, and that he was not God, or that he is only falsely called Son and Lord, then what is this except to make him Yes and No? If things really are as they make them out to be then I think this saying rightly applies to him: "I am what I am by the grace of God" (1 Cor 15:10). For whatever is not a natural property, but is given by someone else as an external addition, is not the property of the one who receives it, but of the one who bestows it as a gift. But if this were so how could he possibly say "I am the truth" (Jn 14:6) if there is nothing true about him? And if he had lied he would have been "overcome by the darkness" (cf. Jn 1:5) but in fact, as it is written, "He did no sin, nor was any deceit found in his mouth" (Is 53:9).

B. Indeed not.

A. Where then is the self-emptying? To whom should we attribute it? One cannot see anyone emptied out there, but on the contrary someone fulfilled, even though he does not have this fullness in his own nature, for if he did have an intrinsic self-perfection and was sufficient in all things he would not have needed what was another's, and it would have been entirely superfluous for him to receive it. Yet, from the fullness of Christ we have all of us received (cf. Jn 1:16) and the preaching of those who were divinely inspired does not lie. Christ, however, was fullness itself and there is absolutely nothing that is given to him insofar as he is considered (and indeed is) God, even if it became his role to receive because of the limitations of the manhood, and insofar as he was revealed like us, to whom it was rightly said: "For what do you have that you did not receive?" (1 Cor 4:7).

B. But they would agree that there is one Christ, and Son and Lord, and conjoined to him is one from the line of David.

A. But, my excellent friends, let me tell you this; if someone has another added to him he cannot be considered one. How could he be? He would be one plus one, or rather one plus someone different, and without any question this makes two. The Son can be truly understood to be one only if we confess that one and the same God the Word is divinely begotten from God, and mysteriously is man born of a woman according to the flesh. But if they set apart and separate out him who is of the line of David, then they surely dismiss him from being Son and God in truth, and maintain instead that he communicates in the sonship and participates in a glory not his own. In that case I think that we will find that the objections the Jews made about him were quite apposite, for they said: "We do not stone you because of a good work, but because of blasphemy, for you who are a man make yourself God" (Jn 10:33).

B. Yet they say that the one Christ is both true God and Son, that is the Word of God who assumes by a conjunction the one who is of David's line.

A. But if the Word of God the Father is not himself the one who is born of a woman according to the flesh, but is different alongside another different person, then how can he be called Christ if he has not been anointed, as we have already said?

B. In that case, if the one who is of the line of David is not different from the Word of God the Father we must admit that he is "before the ages," but then how is it that the all-wise Paul rejects such an opinion when he says, as if posing a question: "Jesus Christ, the same yesterday, and today, and even to the ages?" (Heb 13:8). Putting it another way, what he means is that this Jesus who is the same yesterday and today shall always remain the same, that is "recent," of yesterday and today, whereas God the Word coexists with his own Father.

A. How wrong it is of them to divert the truth to their own absurd personal opinions, and to corrupt the proper meaning of the sacred scriptures. If anyone should say that Christ Jesus is before the ages he would not have departed from the truth, at least if it is true that there is One Son and Lord, the Word who is before the ages who underwent a birth from a woman according to the flesh in the last times of this age. The Word was made man as we are, but was not changed, and the Spirit-bearer testifies to this when he says: "Jesus Christ, the same yesterday, and today, and even to the ages" (Heb 13:8), where the term "yesterday" signifies time past, where "today" signifies present time, and "to the ages" signifies the future and what is to come. They think they have thought up something clever when they take the "yesterday and today" as referring to someone of recent time and then go on to argue adamantly: How can someone who is "yesterday and today" also be "even to the ages"? But we will simply turn the force of the argument around to its direct contrary and ask in reply: How can the Logos, who is "even to the ages," possibly assume to himself something that is "yesterday and today," if it is true that the Christ is one and has not been divided, as the divine Paul tells us (1 Cor 1:13)? As you will understand, this is how he wished to be made known to us. Even when he was visible in the flesh and had entered into the limitations of the manhood he bore witness to his own eternal existence when he said: "Amen I say to you, before Abraham came into being I am" (Jn 8:58), and again: "If I speak to you about earthly realities and you do not believe me, how will you believe me if I tell you of heavenly realities?" (Jn 3:12), and also: "No one has ever gone up into heaven except him who came down from heaven, the Son of Man" (Jn 3:13). So it is as the Word who exists eternally and before the ages, the Word come down from the heavens, the selfsame who appeared as a man like us, that he says these things, as one Christ and Lord, even when he has become flesh.

B. They have discovered another argument, however, which is the following. They maintain that he who is of the line of David should be considered as Son of God in the same way that the Word of God the Father is himself called Son of David, for neither of them are so by nature.

A. In that case let us introduce the manner of the real union so that we may demonstrate what faith teaches about how the Word became flesh, that is man, and was thereby called the Son of David, not in a spurious way, but insofar as he descends from him according to the flesh while remaining what he was, that is God of God. This is what the priests of the evangelical proclamation have taught us about him, for they knew that the same one was at once God and man. So it is written about the blessed Baptist, that: "On the following day he saw Jesus coming towards him and said: Behold the Lamb of God who takes away the sin of the world. This is the one of whom I said: There is coming after me a man who came before me because

he is before me; and I did not know him, yet I came baptising
in water so that he might be revealed to Israel" (Jn 1:29-31).
Note, therefore, how he says he is a man, and calls him a lamb,
and yet he says he is no different to the one who takes away the
sin of the world, and indeed attributes to him this great and truly
vast dignity which befits God. He also says that he came before
and prior to himself, even though he was born after him; I mean
in terms of the date of his birth in the flesh. And so, both the
recent characteristics of humanity, and the eternal characteristics of the deity apply to him. The all-noble Peter gazed
upon the Logos, not nakedly or without flesh, but as he was
revealed in flesh and blood, and he made his tribute of faith in
him clearly and correctly when he said: "You are the Christ,
the Son of the Living God," and he heard in return: "Blessed
are you Simon Bar Jonah because flesh and blood did not reveal
this to you but my Father who is in heaven" (Mt 16:16-17). But
if the mystery was not so deep as this, and he was not in the
flesh, but was rather, as they say, only a man who had the
sonship by grace, then why would Peter have needed such an
initiator, suggesting that no one on earth could reveal this to the
disciple and the Father himself had to be his instructor? The
divine disciples were astounded at the miracle when they saw
him walking over the surface of the sea, and they confessed
their faith saying: "Truly you are the Son of God" (Mt 14:33).
But if he was introduced to the sonship, and is a bastardized
and falsely-named son, then [our opponents] are accusing the
disciples of bearing false witness, for they used the word "truly"
to stress that he is the Son of God the Father.

B. You put it very well indeed.

A. How can the Son of Man have his own angels and shine
out in the glory of his Father [for he says]: "The Son of Man
will come in the glory of his Father with his angels" (Mt 16:7),
and again: "And the Son of Man will send his angels" (Mt

13:41). But if they still refuse to believe when they see him crowned in divine dignity and in these radiant and sublime honors then let them listen to him as he says: "If you do not believe me, believe in my works" (Jn 10:38), and again: "If I do not do the works of my Father then do not believe me, but if I do them, then even if you do not believe me, believe in my works" (Jn 10:37-38). When we see the sublimity of this ineffable glory in a man who does not hold it as belonging to another, nor is offered it in the form of a grace, but has it as his very own, then how can we fail to be persuaded that he was God in our likeness and truly the Son of God who is over all?

B. They would say that he spoke of the angels being his own, and was able to accomplish such signs, because of the Word who dwelt within him and imparted to him his own glory and power as it is written: "Jesus from Nazareth, whom God anointed with the Holy Spirit and with power, who came doing good works and curing all those who lay under the power of the devil" (Acts 10:38). It was from his anointing with power and Spirit, therefore, that he was a wonder-worker.

A. Since the Word is God, however, and is holy by nature and essentially omnipotent, it follows that he will never need either power from someone else, or an imparted holiness, and in that case who is it who is anointed with power and the Holy Spirit?

B. They would doubtless say it was the man assumed into conjunction.

A. Then he is surely Jesus Christ, taken separately and distinctly, of whom the all-wise Paul says: "But for us there is one God, the Father from whom come all things, and we too come from him, and one Lord Jesus Christ, through whom come all things, and we too come through him" (1 Cor 8:6). But then tell me how all things can come through a man? And why is he ranked as Son immediately next to the Father without anyone's mediation? Or where shall we put the Only Begotten after we have elevated the man into his place, a man they tell us who is moved by him and is held in honor because of him? Has not their argument overstepped what is reasonable? Has it not gone beyond the pale? Has it not become utterly ridiculous for having entirely missed the mark as far as truth goes?

B. He would reply that the Word of God is called man in some such fashion: just as the man assumed by him is born in Bethlehem of Judah, and is called a Nazarene because he lived in Nazareth, in the same way God the Word is called man because he dwelt within a man.

A. What a servile mentality from a crazed brain that knows how to do nothing else but gabble. We must reply to our opponents: "You drunken men rouse yourselves from your cups" (Jl 1:5). Why do you do such violence to the truth? Why have you twisted the sense of the divine teachings so as to have been carried off the Royal Road? It would seem that the Word has no longer been made flesh as the scriptures say, but rather an inhabitant of a man, and it follows from this that he should not be called man but should be called "mannish," just as someone who lives at Nazareth is called Nazarene and not Nazareth. But if they think that their foolish inventions are correct, then in my opinion there is absolutely nothing to prevent us from calling the Father and the Holy Spirit a man along with the Son. For the fullness of the consubstantial Trinity dwells within us through the Spirit. This is why Paul says: "Do you not know that you are the temple of God and that the Spirit of God dwells within you?" (1 Cor 3:16). Indeed Christ himself says: "If anyone loves me he will keep my word and my Father will love him, and we shall come to him and make our abode with him" (Jn 14:23). But neither the Father nor the Holy Spirit have ever been called a man because of the fact that they dwell within us. These people are making a mockery of the mystery of the incarnation. Dogmas of the Church which are so right and worthy of being heard are twisted round by them to the point of deformity. Nevertheless, let our discourse proceed once more on its course, bidding farewell to this disgusting mess they have spewed out. For if he became a worker of wonderful signs because the Word was within him, are they not simply saying that he was one of the holy prophets? The Word also worked divine signs through the hands of the saints. If they argue that it is the Son who is in these signs then they have reduced him to the status of the apostles or prophets.

B. They would reply: "But has he not been called Prophet and Apostle?"

A. Well, you are not mistaken. Moses said to the race of Israel, for example: "The Lord your God will raise up for you from among your brethren a prophet like myself" (Acts 3:22; Dt 17:13). And the divine Paul has also written: "And so, holy brethren, sharers in this heavenly calling, consider Jesus the Apostle and High Priest of our confession" (Heb 3:1). However, they must answer this question which I shall pose: Would it be an honor for any man to have the grace of prophecy, or to be endowed with apostolic privileges, or to be called a priest?

B. I would say so.

A. Some might say that considering Christ as God these things are petty and not worth accepting, that they are the way in which he is revealed as having been emptied out, and the things that he takes up along with the manhood. Since he is God and truly Lord by nature, he assumed the form of a slave and he came in this form, adopting our human condition, and then gave the Spirit of prophecy, designated apostles, and established priests. By doing this he was "made like his brethren in all things" (Heb 2:17), and this was why he is named prophet, apostle, and priest.

B. But even if they grant that he was a prophet, they

maintain that he was not just as one of the prophets, rather that he greatly transcended their level. They had grace meted out to them as it seemed fit to God, and it was added to them over time, whereas he was full of the Godhead all at once, from his very birth, for the Word who is God was with him.

A. In that case Christ surpassed the holy prophets who came before him only in terms of the amount of grace and its duration, and this is what constitutes his pre-eminence. But the question which we must address is whether he was a prophet at all, not whether he was a greater or lesser, or even an excelling prophet, for his low degree would consist in the very fact of his being a prophet and in not passing beyond our limitations. This would be the case even if he is understood to be such even from the outset, since this would apply even to the divine Baptist of whom the blessed angel said: "And he shall be filled with the Holy Spirit even from his mother's womb" (Lk 1:15). So how was the one a servant and the other honored with all the dignities of a Lord? Blessed John said this about himself: "He who is of the earth speaks of the earth," but about Emmanuel he says: "He who comes from above is over all" (Jn 3:31).

B. Perhaps they would reply that the Word who has shone forth from God the Father is from above and certainly over all, but they are afraid to attribute human characteristics to him in case he might somehow be dishonored by them, and brought down to a dishonorable state. This is why they maintain that he assumed a man and conjoined him to himself, and that it is to this man that all the human characteristics relate and can be attributed while absolutely no damage is done to the nature of the Word himself.

A. If this were so the one assumed must certainly be understood and confessed to be different from the Word. Still, we will not get involved in the nonsenses of these people, nor shall we make these innovators into the arbiters of our faith, for they set the sacred scripture aside and dishonor the tradition that comes from the holy apostles and evangelists. We ourselves ought not to go astray just because a weak and ignorant mind has taken hold of them, one that cannot look into the depth of the mystery, for otherwise we might become as stupid as them, refusing to go along the straight path of the truth. We know that the all-holy Paul has written that it is necessary "to cast down reasonings and every lofty thought which is raised up against the knowledge of God, and to reduce all conception to captivity in the obedience of Christ" (2 Cor 10:5). Now then, can you tell me which things scandalize them? or what stumbling block have they fallen over like the Jews (1 Cor 1:23)?

B. Indeed I can. How could I not have things to tell? And how many things too, although I will recount them one by one. They say, for example, that Christ has been sanctified by the Father, for it is written: "And John bore witness saying: I have seen the Spirit descending from heaven and it remained upon him. And I did not know him, but he who sent me baptising in water, he it was who said to me: On whoever you shall see the Spirit descending and remaining upon him, he it is who shall baptize in the Holy Spirit. And I have seen, and I have borne witness that this is the Son of God" (Jn 1:32-34). Paul has also written about him: "For the one who sanctifies and those that are sanctified are all of one [origin]" (Heb 2:11). However, since the Logos, who is God and holy by nature, has no need of sanctification, then it only remains to attribute this sanctification to the man assumed by the Word in a conjunction.

A. Then how does he who was baptized, and received the visible descent of the Spirit, himself baptize in the Holy Spirit, or accomplish things which pertain to and are proper to the divine nature alone? For he is the giver of sanctification, and in order to show this was his own proper benefit the Word-made-man physically breathed on his holy apostles saying: "Receive the Holy Spirit. Whoever's sins you forgive they are forgiven, whoever's sins you retain, they are retained" (Jn 20:22-23). And why did the divine Baptist bear witness by saying "This is the Son of God," in the singular and using the definite article, when he was quite obviously referring to the one who had been sanctified? He stood as the initiator of the whole world, and if this was a different son alongside the real son, he knew well enough how to signify the truth, and would have said explicitly: "This is one who has been made a son by gift and grace through his conjunction with him who is true and natural son." He said nothing of the kind, for John knew that he was one and the same, the Word of God the Father and also of David's line according to the flesh. He says that he was sanctified insofar as he was man, but sanctifies insofar as he is understood as God. As I have said, he was both the one and the other in the same [person]. If he had not become man, and had not been born of a woman according to the flesh, then we ought to chase away all human characteristics from him. But if it is true that he abased himself in an emptying-out to become as we are, then why do they deny to him all those things through which he is understood as being emptied out? In this way they have foolishly unravelled the great design of the fleshly economy.

B. So, if he is said to have received glory and to have become Lord, to have been exalted by the Father and established as King, would you attribute even these things to God the Word? If you did would you not thereby utterly dishonor his glory?

A. How could anyone doubt that the nature of God the Word is filled with true and regal dominion? Certainly we must understand this nature as being in the very heights befitting to God. Since he appeared as a man, however, a being upon whom all things are bestowed as gifts, he received as a man, even though he is full and gives to all from his own fullness (Jn 1:16).

He made our poverty his own, and we see in Christ the strange and rare paradox of Lordship in servant's form and divine glory in human abasement. That which was under the yoke in terms of the limitations of manhood was crowned with royal dignities, and that which was humble was raised to the most supreme excellence. The Only Begotten did not become man only to remain in the limits of the emptying. The point was that he who was God by nature should, in the act of self-emptying, assume everything that went along with it. This was how he would be revealed as ennobling the nature of man in himself by making it participate in his own sacred and divine honors. We shall find that even the saints call the Son of God the "Glory" of God the Father, and King, and Lord, even when he became a man. Isaiah, for example, says in one place: "Just as a man gleans an olive tree so shall they be gleaned, and when the harvester leaves off they will raise a shout. Those that are left upon the earth shall rejoice with the glory of the Lord" (Is 24:13-14). And another one of the saints says: "Shine forth Jerusalem for your light has come, and the glory of the Lord has risen upon you. Behold, darkness and gloom may cover the earth, but over you the Lord shall be made manifest and his glory shall be seen upon you" (Is 60:1-2). James, his disciple, says: "Brothers, do not confuse personal preferences with faith in Jesus Christ, our Lord of glory" (Jas 2:1). The divine Peter also says: "If you are reproached in Christ then you are blessed, because the Spirit of God, the Spirit of glory, rests upon you" (1 Pet 4:14)[5]

B. My good friend, this is enough on these matters. Tell us now how we ought to understand the following text which is written of Christ: "Who in the days of his flesh offered prayers and supplications with a great cry and with tears to the one who was able to save him from death. And he was heard because of his godliness, and although he was son he learned obedience

5 Cyril's text differs from all known mss. of the N.T.

from the things he suffered, and being made perfect he became
for those who obey him the cause of their everlasting salvation"
(Heb 5:7-9). I will add to this another saying: "My God, my God,
why have you forsaken me?" (Mt 27:46). They say that such
things are not at all applicable to God the Word, and one might
even argue that they fall far short of his inherent excellence.

A. I too am aware that these things are not at all fitting for
God the Word who issues from God the Father, at least if we
set aside the form of the economy, and if we do not accept that
he "became flesh," in accordance with the scriptures. But since
we make our stand on this point, and since to doubt it would
surely convict us of impiety, then come and let us look into the
profundity of this economy insofar as is possible. The Word of
God the Father, therefore, appeared to us in our likeness,
bringing help to our human condition in myriad ways, and
brilliantly showing us the path which leads to every admirable
thing. But insofar as temptation attacks all those who are put in
danger because of the love of God, then it was necessary for us
to learn how people ought to behave once they have decided to
live an honorable life in exemplary conduct. Should we, for
example, slacken our grip and fall into carelessness, with
unseasonable revelling, living for the sake of pleasure? Or
should we give ourselves over to prayer, standing in tears
before our Savior, seeking and thirsting for his assistance, and
even asking for courage in case it is his will that we should
suffer? Besides, it was also necessary for us to have the bene-
ficial knowledge of how far the limits of obedience should
extend, by what wonderful ways it comes, how great is its
reward, and what form it has. This was the reason Christ
became our model in all these things, and the divine Peter
confirms this for us when he says: "What is so wonderful about
enduring persecution if you have done wrong? But if you have
done good and still must endure, then this is acceptable to God,

for Christ also suffered for you leaving you an example that you might follow in his steps" (1 Pet 2:20-21). And so the Word of God became an example for us in the days of his flesh, but not nakedly or outside the limits of the self-emptying. This was why he was quite properly able to employ the limitations of the manhood. This was why he extended his prayer, and shed a tear, at times even seemed to need a savior himself, and learned obedience, while all the while he was the Son. It was as if the Spirit-bearer [in this passage] was almost astonished at the mystery, that he who was truly and naturally the Son, and eminent in the glories of the Godhead, should bring himself to such abasement as to undergo the abject poverty of the human state. Yet the beautiful and helpful example of this action was for our sake, as I have said. It was meant so that we should learn something from it, an easy lesson, that we must not hurry down another path when the occasion calls for courage. For this reason Christ once said: "Do not be afraid of them that can destroy the body but cannot destroy the soul; be afraid rather of him who is able to destroy both soul and body in Gehenna" (Mt 10:28), and again: "If anyone wishes to come after me let him deny himself, take up his cross, and follow me" (Mt 16:24). What else is involved in the duty of following him other than to overcome temptations manfully by asking for heavenly assistance? We will not do this negligently or carelessly, but only by the most intense prayer when we let the tears of godliness drop from our eyes.

B. How well you put it.

A. So if he said: "My God, my God, why have you forsaken me" (Mt 27:26), how do these people understand it?

B. They would regard these words, I suppose, as coming from the man that was assumed.

A. From a broken man, doubtless, who found the assaults of this trial so hard that it seemed unsupportable? Or how else?

B. They would regard them as the sayings of one who was distraught because of human faintheartedness, or so it would seem. For he also said to his disciples: "My soul is sorrowful even to death" (Mt 26:38), and he fell down before the Father himself saying: "Father, if it is possible, let this chalice pass from me, but not my will, but yours be done" (Mt 26:39).

A. But isn't this exactly the same as what we have spoken of earlier? That is: "Who in the days of his flesh offered prayers and supplications with a great cry, and with tears, to the one who was able to save him from death" (Heb 5:7)? Yet if anyone thinks that Christ had fallen so low into such faintheartedness as to be so "sorrowful and cast down" (Mt 26:37) that he could no longer bear his sufferings but was overcome by fear and mastered by weakness, then he assuredly convicts him of not being God, and also shows that he apparently had no right to rebuke Peter.

B. What do you mean?

A. Well, Christ said: "Behold we are going up to Jerusalem, and the Son of Man shall be betrayed into the hands of sinful men, and they shall mock him and shall crucify him, and on the third day he shall rise again." But then, this lover of God said: "May he be merciful to you Lord, that this shall not happen to you" (cf. Mk 10:34; Mt 16:22). Then what did Christ say to him? "Get behind me Satan for you are a stumbling block to me; for you do not think the things of God but the things of men" (Mt 16:23). How did the disciple make an improper suggestion in wanting this trial to be removed from his master if it was going to prove insufferable for him, and so completely unbearable that it would undoubtedly cast him down into cowardice and break his spirit? After all, he himself had commanded his disciples to stand fast against their fears of death and reckon suffering as nothing in the course of fulfilling the will of God. I am amazed how such people are able to say that such a man has been conjoined to the Only Begotten or go on to maintain that he has shared in the divine dignities when they then subject him to the fears of death and expose him as naked just like any one of us. He presumably gained no benefit at all from his divine dignities?

B. How can we understand the form of the economy in these matters?

A. It is mystical, profound, and truly wonderful, for those who know the mystery of Christ correctly. Look at the sayings which refer to the emptying out, and are accommodated to the limitations of the manhood; look how they come at just the right time, when they are needed, so that he who is above all creation might be revealed as having become like us in all respects. Another conclusion follows from this.

B. Tell me what it is.

A. We had become accursed through Adam's transgression and had fallen into the trap of death, abandoned by God. Yet all things were made new in Christ (2 Cor 5:17) and our condition was restored to what it was in the beginning. It was entirely necessary that the Second Adam, who is from heaven (1 Cor 15:45) and superior to all sin, that is Christ, the pure and immaculate first-fruits of our race, should free that nature of man from judgement, and once again call down upon it the heavenly graciousness of the Father. He would undo our abandonment by his obedience and complete submission: "For he did no sin" (1 Pet 2:22) but the nature of man was made rich in all blamelessness and innocence in him, so that it could now cry out with boldness: "My God, my God, why have you forsaken me?" (Mt 27:46). Understand that in becoming man, the Only Begotten spoke these words as one of us and on behalf of all our nature. It was as if he were saying this: "The first man has transgressed. He slipped into disobedience, and neglected the commandment he received, and he was brought to this state of wilfulness by the wiles of the devil; and then it was entirely

right that he became subject to corruption and fell under judgement. But you Lord have made me a second beginning for all
on the earth, and I am called the Second Adam. In me you see
the nature of man made clean, its faults corrected, made holy
and pure. Now give me the good things of your kindness, undo
the abandonment, rebuke corruption and set a limit on your
anger. I have conquered Satan himself who ruled of old, for he
found in me absolutely nothing of what was his." In my opinion
this is the sense of the Savior's words. He did not invoke the
Father's graciousness upon himself, but rather upon us. The
effects of God's anger passed into the whole of human nature
as from the original rootstock, that is Adam: "For death has had
dominion from Adam up to Moses, even on those who com-
mitted no sin in the manner of Adam's transgression" (Rom
5:14). In the same way, however, the effects of our new
first-fruits, that is Christ, shall again pass into the entire human
race. The all-wise Paul confirms this for us when he says: "For
if many died because of the transgression of one, how much
more" (Rom 5:15) shall many come to life because of the
righteousness of one. And again: "As all men die in Adam, so
shall all be made alive in Christ" (1 Cor 15:22).

B. Do you mean it would be foolish and in complete
disagreement with the sacred scriptures to think or to say that
the assumed man used these human expressions as one who
was abandoned by the Word who had been conjoined to him?

A. My friend, this would be blasphemy, and a proof of
complete madness, but doubtless it would evidently suit those
who do not know how to conceive of the matter properly. They
split up and completely divide his words and acts, attributing
some things as proper solely to the Only Begotten, and others
to a son who is different to him and born of a woman. In this
way they have missed the straight and unerring way of knowing
the mystery of Christ clearly.

B. So in the case of the evangelical and apostolic preaching, one must not divide the words or the acts in this way?

A. Certainly not, at least not as referring to two persons or two hypostases divided from one another and completely diverging into distinct and separate spheres. For there is only one Son, the Word who was made man for our sake. I would say that everything refers to him, words and deeds, both those that befit the deity, as well as those which are human.

B. So even if he is said to have been wearied by the journey (Jn 4:6), to have hungered (Mt 4:2.), and to have fallen asleep (Mt 8:24), would it be proper, tell me, to attribute these things which are petty and demeaning to God the Word?

A. Such things would not be at all fitting to the Word, if we considered him nakedly, as it were, not yet made flesh, or before he he had descended into the self-emptying. Your thoughts are right on this. But once he is made man and emptied out, what harm can this inflict on him? Just as we say that the flesh became his very own, in the same way the weakness of that flesh became his very own in an economic appropriation according to the terms of the unification. So, he is "made like his brethren in all things except sin alone" (Heb 2:17). Do not be astonished if we say that he has made the weakness of the flesh his own along with the flesh itself. He even attributed to himself those external outrages that came upon him from the roughness of the Jews, saying through the voice of the Psalmist: "They divided my garments among them, and cast lots for my clothes" (Ps 22:18), and again: "All those who saw me sneered at me, they wagged their tongues, they shook their heads" (Ps 22:7).

B. Even if perhaps he should say: "Whoever has seen me, has seen the Father. I and the Father are one" (Jn 14:9; Jn 10:3), and then says to the Jews: "Why do you seek to kill me, a man who has spoken to you the truth which I heard from God" (Jn 8:40) then are we to apply both sets of sayings to one and the same subject?

A. Indeed so, for the Christ is in no way divided, but is believed by all those who worship him to be the one and only and true Son. "The image of the unseen God, the brightness of the glory of the Father's hypostasis, the impress of his being" (Col 1:15) "assumed the form of a slave" (Phil 2:6), not as if he joined a man to himself, as they would say, but rather that he himself came in that form, while even so remaining in likeness to God the Father. This was why the all-wise Paul wrote: "Because it is God, he who said that light should shine from darkness, who lit up our hearts for the enlightenment of the knowledge of his glory in the face of Jesus Christ" (2 Cor 4:6). Notice how the radiance of the divine and ineffable glory of God the Father shines "in the face of Jesus Christ." The Only Begotten, even when he has become man, shows forth in himself the glory of the Father. Only in this way, not otherwise, is he understood and designated as Christ. If this is not so let our opponents teach us how one could ever see in an ordinary man the radiance, or even the knowledge, of the divine glory? We do not see God in the form of man; only in the Word who is made man and has become as we are, while ever remaining the true and natural Son (and thus considered in his deity), can we see that this strange reality has come about. Moreover the steward of his mysteries calls him Christ Jesus, since he became as we are and was made flesh, but he knows that at the same time he is naturally and truly God. He writes as follows: "I have written to you more boldly on some points so as to serve as a reminder for you, by virtue of the grace which God gave me that I should be a minister of Christ Jesus for the gentiles in the priestly service of the Gospel of God" (Rom 15:15-16). And Zechariah also prophesies to his own child, that is the Baptist, as follows: "And you, little child, shall be called a prophet of the Most High for you shall go before the face of the Lord to prepare a people for him" (Lk 1:76). Thereafter the divine Baptist pointed out the Most High Lord saying: "Behold the Lamb of God, who takes away the sin of the world. This is the one of whom I said: after me there comes a man who came before me, because he was before me" (Jn 1:29-30). And so, can it be lawful to doubt that the one and only true Son is the Word of God the Father with the flesh he united to himself? This is not a soulless flesh as some would have it, as I have said earlier, but flesh animated with a rational soul, and in all respects one factor (*prosopon*) with it.

B. I do not doubt it in the least, for there is "One Lord, one faith, one baptism" (Eph 4:5). But if Jesus is said to "advance in stature and wisdom and grace" (Lk 2:52) then who is the subject who is "becoming" in this instance? The Word of God the Father is complete and perfect in himself, so what could he progress or advance to? He himself is wisdom, so he cannot be said to receive wisdom [.......................... Manuscript lacuna]. This is why they say that we must seek to discover who it is to whom these things apply.

A. Then it seems that a different Son and Christ and Lord has been introduced, just because certain people are unable to plumb the depths of the sacred scriptures. When the wise evangelist introduces the Word as having been made flesh he shows him economically, allowing his own flesh to obey the laws of its own nature. It belongs to manhood to advance in stature and wisdom, and one might say in grace also, for understanding unfolds in a certain fashion in each person according to the limits of the body. It is one thing in infants, something else in grown children, and something different again for adults. It would not have been impossible, or impractical, for God the Word who issued from the Father to have made that body which he united with himself rise up even from its swaddling bands, and bring it straight to the stature of perfect maturity. One might even say that it would have been plain sailing, quite easy for him to have displayed a prodigal wisdom in his infancy; but such a thing would have smacked of wonder-working, and would have been out of key with the plan of the economy. No, the mystery was accomplished quietly, and for this reason (that is economically) he allowed the limitations of the manhood to have dominion over himself. This was so arranged as part of his "likeness to us," for we advance to greater things little by little as the occasion calls us to assume a greater stature and a concomitant mentality. The Word who is from the Father, then, is entirely perfect and needs nothing whatsoever, since he is God, yet he makes what is ours his own since he became as we are. Even so we know that he is above us, as God. In some places, even though he knows that he became flesh, yet with an eye to the excellencies of the Godhead, Paul even goes so far as to say that he was not even a man. He writes to the Galatians, for instance: "Paul, an apostle, not from man or by a man, but through Jesus Christ" (Gal 1:1). And elsewhere he says: "I declare to you the Good News which I announced, that it is not according to man; for I did not receive it from a man, nor was I taught it. It came by the revelation of Jesus Christ" (Gal 1:11-12).

B. Then should we apply to him what is said about advancing in wisdom and stature and grace, just as as we would with reference to hunger and tiredness and other such things? Perhaps even if he could be said to suffer or be restored to life by the Father we should attribute such things to him as well?

A. We say that these human things are his by an economic appropriation, and along with the flesh all the things belonging to it. We recognize no other Son apart from him, for the Lord himself has saved us, giving his own blood as a ransom for the life of all (Is 63:9 LXX). "We were not bought with a perishable price of silver or gold, but with the precious blood of the spotless lamb without blemish, which is Christ, who offered himself on our behalf as a sweet-smelling offering to God the Father" (cf. 1 Cor 6:20; 1 Pet 1:18-19). And Paul, who was most learned in the law, confirms this for us when he writes: "So become imitators of God as beloved children and walk in love, just as Christ loved us and gave himself up for us as a sweet-smelling offering and sacrifice to God" (Eph 5:1-2). Since Christ has become a sweet odor for our sake, and has revealed in himself the nature of man possessed of sinlessness, then we have had boldness through him and in him towards our God and Father in heaven. It is written: "So brethren, we have the boldness through the blood of Christ to go into the holy places by a new and living way which he has opened for us through the veil, that is his flesh" (Heb 10:19-20). Understand then how he says the flesh is his, and the blood is his, which he also calls "the veil," and rightly so, for what the sacred veil did in the Temple, effectively covering up the Holy of Holies, this is what we can understand the flesh of the Lord does. The Word is made one with it, and in turn it masks the transcendent excellence of the eminence and glory of the Word from being gazed at as if laid bare to the inspection of all. This is exactly why some thought that Christ was "Elijah, and others Jeremiah or one of the prophets" (Mt 16:14). But the Jews who completely misunderstood his mystery spoke badly of him when they said: "Surely this is Jesus, the son of the carpenter? (Mt 13:55) How can he now say: I have come down from heaven" (Jn 6:42)? The deity is invisible by nature, yet he, who in his own nature is not visible, was seen by those on earth in our likeness, and God who is Lord appeared to us. This, I think, is what the divine David teaches us when he says: "God, our God, shall come openly and shall no longer be silent" (Ps 50:3 LXX).

B. You think correctly. They would maintain, however, that things are not like this at all, far from it. They think it is not at all right to attribute the suffering upon the cross to the Word born of God. They would argue instead that he prepared the man who was conjoined to himself in terms of equal honor to undergo the insults of the Jews, and the sufferings on the cross, and even death itself, and that in this way the man became the "leader of our salvation," returning to life and crushing the dominion of death by the power of the Word who was with him.

A. Do they have anything from the sacred scriptures to demonstrate for us the truth of their doctrine on such matters? Or are they innovating in the faith? "Speaking things from their own hearts and not from the mouth of the Lord," as it is written (Jer 23:6). Perhaps they find themselves unable to say: "As for me, let me never boast save in the cross of Christ, through whom the world is crucified to me, and I to the world" (Gal 6:14).

B. They would claim they have [scriptural proofs]; for the all-wise Paul confirms this for us when he writes: "It was fitting for him, because of whom are all things, and through whom are all things, to perfect the leader of their salvation through many sufferings, thus leading many sons to glory" (Heb 2:10). They say that the one in whom are all things, and through whom are all things, can be none other than the Word born of God the Father, and that he, therefore, perfected the leader of our salvation through sufferings, that is the one who is of the line of David.

A. In that case we have no longer been redeemed by God (how could we have been?) but rather by the blood of someone else. Some man or other, an imposter and a falsely-named son, has died for us. The great and venerable mystery of the incarnation of the Only Begotten has turned out to be only words and lies, for he never really became man after all. We certainly could not regard him as our Savior who gave his blood for us, we would have to attribute this to that man. Nonetheless, the most holy Paul wrote to certain persons: "It was necessary, then, that the copies of the heavenly realities should be purified by these things whereas the heavenly realities themselves should be purified by greater sacrifices than these. For Christ did not enter into holy places made by human hands, the figures of the true realities, but into heaven itself, to appear now in the presence of God on our behalf. Nor does he offer himself many times, as the High Priest enters the holy places every year with another's blood, otherwise he would have suffered many times since the foundation of the world. No, he is now made manifest once and for all, in the consummation of the ages, for the abolition of sin through his sacrifice" (Heb 9:23-26). So, if the "type" of the form makes its entrance with another's blood and purifies the people, then the true form, or rather the truth itself, is superior in every respect and the Son enters with his own blood not into some temporary tabernacle made by human hands, a matter of shadows and types, but into that which is above and true, that is into heaven: "For it was necessary that the copies of the heavenly realities should be purified by these things" (Heb 9:23). The former clearly refers to the things that were "symbolic" and "not his own," "whereas the heavenly things themselves should be purified with greater sacrifices than these." This is why we ought to find out what it is in Christ that is greater than the types, I mean what is true, which is "in his own blood."

B. You put it well.

A. They have set up the apostolic saying against us as though it referred only to a common man. Now let us take the quotation from its beginning to the point relevant to our case. Thus it is written: "For we behold Jesus, who for a short time was brought lower than the angels because of the suffering of death, now crowned with honor and glory. It was fitting for him, because of whom are all things, and through whom are all things, to perfect the leader of their salvation through many sufferings, thus leading many sons to glory. For the one sanctifying and those that are sanctified are all of one [origin], and this is why he is not ashamed to call them brothers, saying: I announced your name to my brethren, or again: Behold, I and the children which God gave me... And since the children have fellowship in flesh and blood he too equally shared in these things so that through death he could destroy the one who has the power of death, that is the devil, and should deliver those who through all their lives had been held in bondage by the fear of death. He did not take his descent from angels but from Abraham. Hence in all things he ought to be made like his brethren" (Heb 2:9, 10-17). So notice then, observe how very clearly he says that he was brought lower than the angels through the suffering of death, and that he has thereby "been crowned with honor and glory," and yet he makes it obvious to whom his words refer, clearly the Only Begotten. He tells us that "he shared in flesh and blood equally with us" and that "he did not take his descent from angels but from Abraham," because it was pleasing to God the Father, "because of whom are all things, and through whom are all things," to perfect the Son through sufferings when he descended into the self-emptying and was made man, that is when he took the form of a slave and consecrated his own flesh as a ransom for the life of all. The Christ has been sanctified for us as a spotless oblation, and "by one offering he has perfected those who were to be sanctified for ever" (Heb 10:14) and has refashioned the nature of man into what it was in the beginning. "In him all things are made new" (2 Cor 5:17). The all-wise Paul confirms that God the Father has given his own son for our sake when he writes: "He did not spare his own son but gave him up on behalf of us all, so how could he not grant us all things along with him" (Rom 8:32)? We say, then, that the Word who shines forth from God's essence is his proper Son, but that he is not given on behalf of us nakedly, as it were, or as yet without flesh, but rather when he became flesh. To say that he suffered does no disgrace to him, for he did not suffer in the nature of the godhead, but in his own flesh. God the Father, as I said earlier, "made him who knew no sin into sin for our sake, in order that we might become the righteousness of God along with him" (2 Cor 5:21).

B. Ought we to consider that he actually became sin, or rather that he was made like to those who are under sin, and for this reason is said to be sin?

A. You express it correctly. Just as "he made him who knew no sin into sin for our sake that we might become the righteousness of God in him" (for the nature of man has been justified in him), so in the same way he caused him who knew not death (since the Word is life and life-giver) to suffer in the flesh. But insofar as he is considered as God he remained outside suffering in order that we might live through him and in him. For this reason the suffering of Christ has been called "the likeness of death". So it is written: "If we become one being with him in the likeness of his death, so shall we be of his resurrection" (Rom 6:5). The Word was alive even when his holy flesh was tasting death, so that when death was beaten and corruption trodden underfoot the power of the resurrection might come upon the whole human race. It is a fact that "just as in Adam all men die, so all men shall be made alive in Christ" (1 Cor 15:22). How else should we say that the mystery of the economy of the Only Begotten in the flesh brought help to the nature of man, except that he who is above all creation brought himself down into a self-emptying and lowered himself in our condition? How else could it be except that the body which lay under corruption became a body of life so as to become beyond death and corruption?

B. Is this why we say that the Word of God the Father himself suffered in the flesh for our sake?[6]

6 This defends Cyril's 12th "Anathema" attached to his Third Letter (Ep. 17).

A. Exactly so, at least if Paul is truthful when he says: "He is the image of the invisible God, the first-born of all creation, for all things were created in him, visible and invisible, whether Thrones, or Dominions, or Principalities, or Powers; all things were created through him and for him. He is before all things, and in him all things hold together. He is the head of the body, the church. He is the beginning, the first-born from the dead, that in all things he might be pre-eminent" (Col 1:15-18). So take note, and observe how very clearly he says that it is the image of the unseen God, the first-born of all creation visible and invisible, through whom are all things and in whom are all things, who has been given as a head to the church, and who is also the first-born from the dead. As I have said, he made the characteristics of his flesh his very own and "endured the cross, despising the shame" (Heb 12:2). We do not say that a simple man honored in conjunction with him (how, I know not) was given on our behalf, rather that the Lord of Glory is himself the crucified one, as it is written: "If they had known they would not have crucified the Lord of Glory" (1 Cor 2:8). He suffered in the flesh for us, and on our behalf, "who is of the Jews according to the flesh, God over all blessed for ever" (cf. Rom 9:5). This is how the most holy Paul has written, that herald and apostle who had the very Christ within himself. But, tell me this, when Christ says to the Samaritan woman: "You worship what you do not know. We worship what we do know, for salvation is of the Jews" (Jn 4:22), then how do these people understand such a text, given that "it was no elder or angel that saved us, but the Lord himself" (Is 63:9), and not by another's death, or through the mediation of a common man, but by his own blood? How rightly the all-wise Paul said: "Anyone who sets aside the law of Moses is put to death without mercy at the hands of two or three witnesses. How much more severe do you think would be the punishment of anyone who tramples underfoot the Son of God, considers the blood of the new covenant a common thing, and scorns the spirit of grace in which he was sanctified" (Heb 10:28-29)? Yet if it was not really the precious blood of the true Son made man, but rather of some bastard son different from him, someone who holds the sonship by grace, then how could one fail to conclude that it really was a common thing? So, even if he is said to suffer in the flesh, even so he retains his impassibility insofar as he is understood as God. The divine Peter also says: "Christ died for us once and for all, on behalf of our sins, the righteous for the unrighteous, that he might lead us to God. Put to death in the flesh, he was made alive in the spirit" (1 Pet 3:18). I suppose someone might ask why did the spirit-bearer not say simply and straightforwardly here that he suffered, but added on the words "in the flesh"? He knew, you see, he knew that he was speaking about God, and so he attributed impassibility to him insofar as he is understood as God, adding on, most skillfully, "in the flesh," which is, of course, where the suffering occurs.

B. They argue that to have to say that the same one suffers and does not suffer makes it seem like a fairy tale, and indeed verges on the incredible. For either, as God, he has not suffered at all, or alternatively, if he is said to have suffered, then how can he be God? For such reasons the one who suffers must be understood to be only the one who is of David's line.

A. Is not this an evident demonstration of their feebleness of mind to choose to say and think this? God the Father did not give us any common man taken up in the rank of mediator and artificially holding the glory of sonship, honored with the conjunction of a relationship; no, he gave him who is above all creation, who for our sake came in our likeness, the Word who issues from his own being, so that he might be seen as the equivalent of the life of all. In my opinion it is the height of absurdity, as I have already said, to find fault with the Only

Begotten, when he did not disdain the economy and became flesh, and accuse him of having militated against his own glory by choosing inappropriately to suffer in the flesh. My good friend, this was a matter of the salvation of the whole world. And since on this account he wished to suffer, even though he was beyond the power of suffering in his nature as God, then he wrapped himself in flesh that was capable of suffering, and revealed it as his very own, so that even the suffering might be said to be his because it was his own body which suffered and no one else's. Since the manner of the economy allows him blamelessly to choose both to suffer in the flesh, and not to suffer in the Godhead (for the selfsame was at once God and man) then our opponents surely argue in vain, and foolishly debase the power of the mystery, when they think they have made a worthy synthesis. It seems that the fact he so chose to suffer in the flesh was somehow blameworthy of him, but in another way it was glorious, for the resurrection has testified that he is greater than death and corruption. As God he is life and life-giver, and so he raised up his own temple. This is why the divine Paul said: "I am not ashamed of the Gospel since it is the power of God for the salvation of everyone who believes" (Rom 1:16), and again: "The message of the cross is foolishness for those that are perishing, but to those of us who are saved it is the power of God, and to those who are called, Jews as well as Greeks, it is Christ, the power and the wisdom of God" (1 Cor 1:18, 24). When the Son himself was about to go up to his saving Passion he also said: "Now is the Son of Man glorified, and God is glorified in him, and God shall glorify him in himself and shall glorify him straightway" (Jn 13:31-32). Indeed, having despoiled Hell he returned to life, and not after any long period but "straightway," as it were, and on the very heels of the Passion.

B. Does not the all-wise Paul also say: "Yet you seek a proof that it is Christ who speaks in me, he who is not weak but powerful among you. Though indeed he was crucified out of weakness he lives now from the power of God" (2 Cor 13:3-4).

A. Do we not say over and over again that the Word of God was made flesh and became man?

B. Yes, and how could it be otherwise?

A. Well then, it is the one "who is weak" in the flesh, insofar as he was revealed as man who "lived from the power of God," a power indeed not alien to him but integral, since he actually was God in the flesh.

B. Yet the Father is said to have raised him, for it is written: "According to the working of that power of his might which he worked in the Christ, raising him from the dead and sitting him at his right hand in the heavenly places, above every name that can be named" (Eph 1:19-21).

A. We say that he is the life-giving power of the Father, and that he is naturally resplendent in all the dignities of the one who begot him, even when he became flesh. He himself can stand as his own witness here when he says: "For just as the Father gives life to whomsoever he wills, so does the Son give life to anyone he wills" (Jn 5:21). And he is quite able to do this effortlessly, for he addressed the Jewish people as follows: "Destroy this temple and in three days I shall raise it" (Jn 2:19). Yet he who rose again sat "upon the right hand of the Father in the heavenly places, above every Principality, and Authority, and Dominion, and every name that can be named" (Eph 1:20-21). So is this a different son to the Word who issued from him? Someone who is honored because of a mere conjunction, who receives the title of Godhead by the lot of grace? Or is it not rather the one who is truly and naturally the Son, the one who "came in the likeness of men and was found in fashion as a man" (Phil 2:7) in an economic manner?

B. They would say, perhaps, that it was only the man of the

line of David who was conjoined to him in an equality of honor who could appropriately suffer death.

A. But as I have already said, something which is said to be "equal in honor" to something else cannot be numerically one with it; rather it is one alongside another. This, I think, makes two things which are unequal in nature, at least if the one that is honored is less than the one who honors. Given that only one son sat down at the right hand, let them teach us who it is who has been honored with these heavenly thrones, and sits alongside the Father, since it would be a most dreadful thing to dare to hold a slave in the selfsame honor as the master, or a creature in the same honor as the Creator, or one under the yoke with the King of all, or one ranked among all with the one who transcends all.

B. Then explain this for us a little further.

A. Well, I think that our discourse has already treated these matters sufficiently and clearly enough but, alright, I will add a few other things without hesitation to what I have already said. I will not take up this fight for the sacred dogmas mean-spiritedly; no, I shall raise up the truth in full battle array against those who think perversities. He himself confirms that it was the Only Begotten Word of God who has destroyed the dominion of death; not a different son to him joined in a relationship to mediate this economy, but he himself, personally. He confirms this when he says: "God so loved the world that he gave his Only Begotten Son so that everyone who believes in him might have eternal life" (Jn 3:16). When God the Father so exalts his love for the world, explaining how immensely great and vast it is, then why do our opponents so belittle it, saying that it was not the true Son who was given for us? They introduce in place of the natural Son someone else who is like us and has the sonship as a grace; but it really was the Only Begotten who was given for our sake. John wisely wrote: "The

Only Begotten God, he who is in the bosom of the Father" (Jn 1:18), so how can we not marvel at their stupidity when they cast out the Only Begotten Word of God from the economy in order to bring in, as I have said, someone alien, endowed with external glories, who has the title of godhead laid upon him?

What will then be left of the great and admirable love of the Father if he only gave up a part of the world for its sake, and a small part at that? Perhaps it would not even be wrong to say that the world was redeemed without God's help, since it was served in this respect from within its own resources?

B. They say that the Only Begotten has been given by the Father so as to put our affairs in order, not that he should suffer the things of man in his own nature, since this would be impossible.

A. In his own nature he certainly suffers nothing, for as God he is bodiless and lies entirely outside suffering. On his own testimony, however, and I mean what he said through the lyre of the Psalmist, a body was prepared for him by the Father, and then he came in that body to do the Father's will (cf. Ps 40:6-8 LXX). This will was no less than the redemption through the honorable cross, and the recapitulation of all things, something that was perfectly accomplished through him and in him. The most excellent Paul supports what I have said when he writes: "Let each of you have this mind among you which was in Christ Jesus, who though he was in the form of God did not consider equality with God a thing to be grasped, but emptied himself out, assuming the form of a slave, and coming in the likeness of men, and being found in fashion as a man he humbled himself and became obedient even to death, death on a cross. For this reason God has highly exalted him and granted him the name above every name, that in the name of Jesus every knee should bend, of those in heaven, on the earth, and in the underworld, and every tongue should confess that Jesus Christ is Lord to the glory of God the Father" (Phil 2:5-11). So who would you say is the one who is in the form of God the Father? Who is it who could have remained in equality with him yet did not think this pre-eminent and divine dignity and this transcendence of all things something to be grasped? Is it not God the Word who issues from him? If so, how is the matter not evident to all? It is he who was "in the form of God," the one who was equal with God, who assumed the "form of a slave," and not in the manner of a conjunction of relationship but rather as "coming in the likeness of men and being found in fashion as a man." Yet even so he was God and "he humbled himself and became obedient to death, death on a cross."

B. They would argue that scripture says of him: "God granted him the name above every name so that in the name of Jesus every knee should bend"; but how could the Word ever be understood as receiving something which he already was, being God? And this is why it is necessary to say that the name above every name was given rather to the man who was assumed, and then we will not be guilty of thinking anything unseemly of the Only Begotten.

A. In that case would it not be incomparably better to say that the name was given by the Father to the natural son who was made man for our sake, so that even in the manhood he might be understood to be God, and though he endured the abasement of our condition, to be in the most transcendent heights? In this way we will not introduce any new or recent god among angels and men, one that holds the glory of the Godhead not essentially within his own being, but as something added on from outside, and as if only by the will of God the Father.

B. Then should we conclude that the "name above every name" was given by God the Father to the Word who was born from him?

A. Indeed so. And our argument is not off the mark in this respect, at least if it is true that "he did not consider equality with God a thing to be grasped" but descended into a condition without glory insofar as he was revealed as man. This is why he said: "The Father is greater than I," even though he had the right to have exact equality with him in all things and to rejoice in the glory of the Godhead since he has existed with God eternally insofar as he is conceived as, and actually is, God. We must not think that he who descended into the limitation of manhood for our sake lost his inherent radiance and that transcendence that comes from his nature. No, he had this divine fullness even in the emptiness of our condition, and he enjoyed the highest eminence in humility, and held what belongs to him by nature (that is, to be worshipped by all) as a gift because of his humanity. Every knee bends before him, "those in heaven and those on earth," and every rank proclaims his praise, for Jesus Christ is believed on as Lord "to the glory of God the Father." This is why he said to God the Father in heaven: "Father glorify me with that glory which I had with you before the world was" (Jn 17:5). So tell me, did this man whom they say was assumed by the Only Begotten in a conjunction of relationship pre-exist the world?

B. Not at all.

A. Who is it then who is asking for the glory which he says existed in himself before the very foundation of the world, since he was always and ever with God? Was it not God the Word who is co-eternal with the Father, who shares his throne and co-exists with him? The all-wise evangelist John said of him: "The Word was with God, and the Word was God" (Jn 1:1).

B. How could it be otherwise?

A. Just as he is the Lord of Glory and then abases himself into the low status of the slave's form, so he asks to take up his eternally inherent glory again, and he does this in a way that befits a man. Since he is eternally God he ascends from the limitations of our condition to the pre-eminence and glory of his own Godhead so that every knee should bend before the one true and natural Son, albeit as I have said, one who is made flesh and has become as we are. In my opinion, if we think and believe this we shall abolish from heaven and earth every charge of man-worshipping; for it is written: "You shall worship the Lord your God and adore him alone" (Mt 4:10).

B. This argument needs much more support, so please continue and clarify the mystery for us through some other ideas.

A. I will surely do so, and very gladly. I would say that they have missed the truth when they yoke together a different son who is of David's line with the true and natural Son, that is the Only Begotten. Does not sacred scripture clearly shout out: "The first man is of the earth, and earthly, the second is from heaven" (1 Cor 15:47)? And does not the Son himself say: "For I have come down from heaven not to do my own will but the will of the one who sent me. And this is the will of the one who sent me that of all that he has given me I should lose nothing, but that I should raise it up on the last day" (Jn 6:38-39)? Whom then do they say is this one who has come down from heaven? For as far as the body was concerned it was evidently born of a woman.

B. Obviously it was the Word begotten of God the Father, for I suppose they would not choose to think anything other than this.

A. Quite so, my friend. Yet the all-wise John writes somewhere: "He who comes from above, is above all" (Jn 3:31). So, insofar as the Father wishes to raise up all that he has given to him, an act which is both good and godly, since it is fitting to God to save, then how is it that he says he came down not to do his own will but that of the Father? Should anyone of us think that the Son who is born from God the Father lags behind him in clemency or is so poorer than him in goodness that it is not pleasing to him to abolish corruption from men?

B. I can see the risk of that.

A. We should quite properly argue that since he is the genuine offspring of the Good Father, he himself ought to be understood as good, or rather goodness itself: "For from the fruit you shall know the tree" (Mt 12:33), as he himself said. So, what he says is proven true: "He who has seen me has seen the Father. I and the Father are one" (Jn 14:9; 10:30).

B. You put it well, but please clarify what seems obscure here.

A. We say that the destruction of death and the banishing of corruption from the bodies of men was certainly something that the Son wanted to do. As it is written: "He takes no delight in the destruction of the living, but the generations of the world are preserved" (Wis 1:13-14). " Yet through the envy of the devil death entered into our world" (Wis 2:24). But there was no other way to shake off the gloomy dominion of death, only by the incarnation of the Only Begotten. This was why he appeared as we are and made his own a body subject to corruption according to the inherent system of its nature. In so far as he himself is life, for he was born from the life of the Father, he intended to implant his own benefit within it, that is life itself. Once he had chosen to undergo likeness to us, out of his compassion and loving-kindness towards us, then it was also necessary to submit to suffering when the wickedness of the Jews was unleashed against him. The shamefulness of his Passion was nonetheless a burden for him, and when the time came when it was necessary to endure the cross on behalf of the life of all, he approached it in a way befitting a man, in the fashion of prayer. This was to show that he did not look forward to the passion, and thus he said: "Father, if it is possible, let this chalice pass from me; but not my will but yours be done" (Mt 26:39). He is saying that he who is from heaven did not descend unwillingly to do what would cause him grief, but descended so that he might restore the resurrection to those on earth, something he alone had formed afresh for human nature since he became "the first-born from the dead" according to the flesh, and the "first-fruits of those who have fallen asleep" (cf. Col 1:18; 1 Cor 15:20).

B. Are we, then, to attribute the suffering to him and to no other, insofar as he appeared as a man, even if he remained impassible insofar as he is understood as God?

A. That is exactly what I am saying. Remember that the God-inspired scripture says: "The first man, Adam, was made a living soul; the last Adam a life-giving spirit" (1 Cor 15:45).

B. Should we say, then, that the Word of God has been called the Last Adam?

A. This is true, as I have said, not "nakedly," but rather when he has come in our likeness. Then we say that he is the Last Adam insofar as to give life is not a human act, but rather something that befits God. He also has this title since he came from Adam according to the flesh, as a second beginning for those on earth, to transform the nature of man in himself into a newness of life in holiness and incorruptibility through the resurrection from the dead. This was how death was destroyed since life "naturally" did not allow its own body to endure corruption since it was not possible for the Christ to be under its dominion according to the words of the divine Peter (Acts 2:24). This was how the benefit of this achievement passed over even to us.

B. How excellently you put it.

A. But consider now this fact too.

B. What do you mean?

A. Somewhere Christ said to his holy apostles: "Go forth and make disciples of all nations, baptizing them in the name of the Father, and of the Son, and of the Holy Spirit" (Mt 28:19). We are baptized, therefore, into the holy and consubstantial Trinity; I mean into the Father and the Son and the Holy Spirit. Or is what I have said not correct?

B. How could it be otherwise?

A. Do we not consider as Father, the one who has begotten, and on the other hand consider as Son the Only Begotten Word of God who is born from him by nature?

B. Indeed so.

A. Then how are we baptized into his death, according to the saying of the blessed Paul who tells us: "For those of us who were baptized into Christ were baptized into his death" (Rom 6:3). And yet "there is one Lord, one faith, one baptism" (Eph 4:5), and he certainly would not say that we were baptized into someone who was a distinctly different son of the line of David. Since he is God by nature, he is conceived of as beyond suffering, and then he chose to suffer so that he might save those under corruption, and so became like those on earth in all respects, and underwent birth from a woman according to the flesh. As I have said, he made his very own a body capable of tasting death and capable of coming back to life again, so that he himself might remain impassible and yet be said to suffer in his own flesh. In this way he saved what was lost (Mt 18:11) and openly said: "I am the Good Shepherd. The Good Shepherd lays down his own life for the sake of the sheep." And again: "No one takes my life from me; I lay it down of my own accord. I have the authority both to lay it down and to take it up" (Jn 10:11,18). It does not pertain to any one of us, nor to any common man, to have the authority to lay down his life and take it up again. Yet the Only Begotten and True Son has laid it down and taken it up again, thereby pulling us out of the

snares of death. One can also see this very clearly in the books
of Moses, figured there as if in shadows for those of ancient
times. Then the sacrifice of the sheep rescued the Israelites from
death and corruption, and averted the Destroyer. This was a
type of Christ: "For Christ our Passover was sacrificed for us"
(1 Cor 5:7) that he might undo the gloomy dominion of death
and might gain possession of all that is under heaven by his
own blood. "We were bought at a price" and "are not our own"
(1 Cor 6:19, 20) because "one died on behalf of all" (he who is
more worthy than all) "so that those who live should no longer
live for themselves but for the one who died on their behalf and
rose again" (2 Cor 5:15). Paul confirms this when he says:
"Through the law I died to the law that I might live to God. I
am crucified with Christ. Now it is no longer I who live but
Christ who lives in me. And the life that I now live in the flesh,
I live in the faith of the Son of God who loved me and gave
himself for me" (Gal 2:19-20). So, we are all Christ's, and
through him who suffered in the flesh for our sake we are
reconciled to the Father so that he might reveal us as having
been purified. Thus it is written: "For this reason Jesus suffered
outside the gate so that he might sanctify the people through
his own blood" (Heb 13:12), and again: "We who were once
estranged and enemies in our mentality and our evil works, he
has now reconciled in his own fleshly body through his death,
to present us as holy and blameless before him" (Col 1:21-22).
Note how he says it was "his own body" and "his own flesh"
which was given up for us. We must not say, then, that the flesh
and blood was that of another son apart from him, understood
as separate and honored by a mere conjunction, having an alien
glory, someone who did not have pre-eminence substantially,
but only as if the name of sonship and that of Godhead which
is above every name were thrown over him like a mask [7] or a

7 Lit. "as something prosopic."

cloak. If he were like this, and had such a nature as our opponents have imagined him to have, then it would be entirely unfitting for him to say: "I am the truth" (Jn 14:6). How can that be true which is not what it is said to be, but is really something falsely named and bastardized? But Christ is truth, and, as God, is over all. The Word remained what he was even when he became flesh, so that he who is over all, and yet came among all through his humanity, should keep in himself his transcendence of all and remain above all the limitations of the creation.

B. We would argue that one inflicts a terrible dishonor on the Word of God if one says that he suffered, and that this brings our noble mystery into disrepute.

A. Well, "despising the shame" he chose to "suffer in the flesh" for our sake, according to the scripture (Heb 12:2; 1 Pet 4:1), and in my opinion he must evidently have the problem of a Jewish mentality or the culpable stupidity of the Greeks if he thinks that the suffering on the cross was anything to be ashamed of. The divine Paul wrote of this: "Though the Jews ask for signs, and the Greeks search for wisdom, yet we proclaim a crucified Christ; a stumbling block for the Jews, and foolishness to the gentiles, but to those who are called, Jews as well as Greeks, Christ the power of God and the wisdom of God; because the foolishness of God is wiser than men and the weakness of God is stronger then men" (1 Cor 1:22-25).

B. How can this be? I really do not understand.

A. Does he not say that the suffering on the cross became a stumbling block for the Jews and a foolishness for the Greeks? When they saw him hanging on the wood the former shook their murderous heads against him and said: "If you are the Son of God come down from the cross and we shall believe in you" (Mt 27:40). They thought that he was beaten by their power and so had been seized and crucified; but they were mistaken, for they did not think that he really was the Son of God. They were looking at the flesh. The Greeks, on the other hand, are wholly incapable of grasping the profundity of the mystery, for they think it is foolishness on our part to say that Christ died for the life of the world. Yet this very thing which seems to be foolishness is that which is "wiser than men." This system concerning Christ the Savior of us all is very profound and truly full of heavenly wisdom. What the Jews think of as weakness is far stronger than men; for the Only Begotten Word of God has saved us by putting on our likeness. Suffering in the flesh, and rising from the dead, he revealed our nature as greater than death or corruption. What he achieved was beyond the ability of our condition, and what seemed to have been worked out in human weakness and by suffering was really stronger than men and a demonstration of the power that pertains to God.

B. But they say, how can the same one both suffer and not suffer?

A. He suffers in his own flesh, and not in the nature of the Godhead. The method of these things is altogether ineffable, and there is no mind that can attain to such subtle and transcendent ideas. Yet, following these most correct deductions, and carefully considering the most reasonable explanations, we do not deny that he can be said to suffer (in case we thereby imply that the birth in the flesh was not his but someone else's), but this does not mean that we say that the things pertaining to the flesh transpired in his divine and transcendent nature. No, as I have said, he ought to be conceived of as suffering in his own flesh, although not suffering in any way like this in the Godhead. The force of any comparison falters here and falls short of the truth, although I can bring to mind a feeble image of this reality which might lead us from something tangible, as it were, to the very heights and to what is beyond all speech. It is like iron, or other such material, when it is put in contact with a raging fire. It receives the fire into itself, and when it is in the very heart of the fire, if someone should beat it, then the material itself takes the battering but the nature of the fire is in no way injured by the one who strikes. This is how you should understand the way in which the Son is said both to suffer in the flesh and not to suffer in the Godhead. Although, as I said, the force of any comparison is feeble, this brings us somewhere near the truth if we have not deliberately chosen to disbelieve the holy scriptures.

B. Well said.

A. If the flesh that is united to him, ineffably and in a way that transcends thought or speech, did not become the very flesh of the Word, directly, then how could it be understood as life-giving? He himself says: "I am the living bread which has come down from heaven and gives life to the world. If anyone should eat of this bread he shall live forever, and the bread which I shall give is my flesh for the life of the world" (Jn 6:51,33). But if it is the flesh of a different son than him, someone appropriated by him in a conjunction of relationship, called to an equality of honor as a grace, then how can he call this his own flesh if he is ignorant of all deceit? And how could the flesh of anyone else ever give life to the world if it has not become the very flesh of Life, that is of him who is the Word of God the Father? The divine said of him: "And we know that the Son of God has come and has given us understanding that we might know him, and we are in his true Son Jesus Christ. This is the true God, and life everlasting" (1 Jn 5:20).

B. I suppose they would say in reply that he also quite clearly said: "Amen, Amen, I say to you, unless you eat the flesh of the Son of Man and drink his blood, you shall not have life within you" (Jn 6:53). They say that we should understand from this that the honorable body and blood are not those of God the Word but those of the man assumed by him.

A. Then where do they locate "the great mystery of piety"?

(1 Tim 3:16), for it seems that the self-emptying of God the Word is destroyed, who though he was in the form and equality of the Father chose to assume the form of a slave for our sake, and came in likeness to us, and shared in flesh and blood, and graced everything under heaven with the economy of the incarnation. This is how salvation came about with the Father recapitulating all things in him, "things in heaven and things on earth" as it is written (Eph 1:10). If they say that this is not the Only Begotten who speaks at once in human and divine fashion when he says: "And the bread which I shall give is my flesh for the life of the world" (Jn 6:51) rather that it was some Son of Man conceived of as different and separate from him who saved us, then it is no longer "the Lord himself who saved us," as it is written (Is 63:9 LXX), but one of our own number, and in that case all those who are subject to corruption are not brought to life by God (who does have the power to bring to life) but by one who is subject to corruption himself, someone who receives life as a gift along with us. On the other hand if it is true that the Word became flesh, in accordance with the scriptures, and "appeared on the earth and had converse with men" (Bar 3:37), taking the form of a slave as his very own, then he can also be called the Son of Man; and if certain people feel ashamed of this, they thereby expose themselves to the charge of stupidity. There was no other way for the flesh to become life-giving, even though by its own nature it was subject to the necessity of corruption, except that it became the very flesh of the Word who gives life to all things. This is exactly how it accomplishes his own ends, working by his own life-giving power. There is nothing astonishing here, for if it is true that fire has converse with materials which in their own natures are not hot, and yet renders them hot since it so abundantly introduces to them the inherent energy of its own power, then surely in an even greater degree the Word who is

God can introduce the life-giving power and energy of his own self into his very own flesh. We can see that this is his very own flesh since he is united to it unconfusedly and unchangeably and in a manner he alone knows.

B. Then must we confess that it has become entirely the personal body of the Word of the Father with no one else intervening, even though it is understood as animated with a rational soul?

A. Exactly so, if we are to define the doctrine of faith correctly and without error, and are lovers of the doctrines of the truth, who follow in the track of the faith of our holy fathers. In this way we shall not be carried away from the right path, and will not abandon the royal road, by being carried off into a debased mentality by the empty myths of certain people. No, we shall be built upon the foundation stone itself, that is Christ: "For no one is able to lay any other foundation apart from that already in position" (1 Cor 3:10-11), as the wise architect and priest of his mysteries has so truly written. This is why we believe that there is only one Son of God the Father. This is why we must understand Our Lord Jesus Christ in one person.[8] As the Word he is born divinely before all ages and times, but in these last times of this age the same one was born of a woman according to the flesh. To the same one we attribute both the divine and human characteristics, and we also say that to the same one belongs the birth and the suffering on the cross since he appropriated everything that belonged to his own flesh, while ever remaining impassible in the nature of the Godhead. This is why "every knee shall bend before him, and every tongue shall confess that Jesus Christ is Lord, to the glory of God the Father" (Phil 2:10-11).

—Amen.

8 *prosopon.*

SELECT BIBLIOGRAPHY

A. *Texts and Translations of St Cyril*

Cyril's Writings:

A fully detailed account of Cyril's writings can be found in *Clavis Patrum Graecorum*, vol. III., ed. M. Geerard (Turnhout, 1979), pp. 5200-5438.

Explanations of the contents of Cyril's treatises and bibliographical data (valid up to the mid-seventies) is provided in an excellent survey by Johannes Quasten, *Patrology*, vol.3. The Golden Age of Greek Patristic Literature (Utrecht/Antwerp, 1975), pp. 116-142.

Primary Sources:

The best critical text for most of the Cyrilline literature relating to the christological controversy is that of:

E. Schwartz, *Acta Conciliorum Oecumenicorum. Concilium Universale Ephesinum*, Bk. I, vols. 1-5 (Berlin/Leipzig, 1927-1930).

The works of Cyril can also be found in:

J.P. Migne, *Patrologiae Cursus Completus: Series Graeca* (PG) vols. 68-77, 1st ed. (Paris, 1859) (reprint Turnhout, 1991).

P.E. Pusey published seven volumes of critical editions of the biblical commentaries of Cyril including (Latin Titles):

Commentary on the Twelve Prophets (Oxford, 1868); *Commentary on The Gospel of John* (Oxford, 1872); *Various Christological Treatises* (Oxford 1875-1877).

The Syriac version of Cyril's Commentary on Luke was published by:

J.B. Chabot, *Corpus Scriptorum Christianorum Orientalium*, vol. 70 (Paris, 1912) (Latin Translation by R. Tonneau, CSCO 140 [Louvain, 1953]).

Other Syriac fragments can be found in the collected works of Severus of Antioch, collated by:

J. Lebon, CSCO 93-94, 101-102, 111-112, & 119-120.

More recently R.Y. Ebied and Lionel Wickham have edited and published new Syriac discoveries:

R.Y. Ebied & L.R. Wickham, "A Collection of Unpublished Syriac Letters of Cyril of Alexandria," CSCO, vols. 359-360 (Louvain, 1975).

_____, "The Letter of Cyril of Alexandria to Tiberius the Deacon. Syriac Version." *Le Muséon* 83, 433-482.

_____, "An Unknown Letter of Cyril of Alexandria in Syriac," JTS (NS) 22 (1971), 420-443.

The most recent critical editions of Cyril's dogmatic works are those in the *Sources Chrétiennes* series (with a French translation and excellent introductory studies) by:

G. M. De Durand, *Cyrille d'Alexandrie. Deux Dialogues Christologiques,* SC 97 (Paris, 1964).

_____, *Cyrille d'Alexandrie: Dialogues sur la Trinité*, SC 231, 237 and 246 (Paris, 1976, 1977, 1978).

P. Burguiere and P. Evieux, *Cyrille D'Alexandrie: Contre Julien*, SC 322 (Paris, 1985).

English Translations of Works by Cyril:

R. Payne-Smith, *A Commentary Upon the Gospel According to S. Luke by Cyril, Patriarch of Alexandria*, 2 vols. (Oxford, 1859).

P. E. Pusey, *The Three Epistles of St Cyril. (The Dogmatic Letters to Nestorius)* (Oxford, 1872).

_____, *The Commentary on St John*, vol. 1. Library of Fathers of the Church 43 (Oxford, 1874).

_____, *That The Christ is One*, Library of Fathers of the Church 46 (Oxford, 1881).

_____, *Five Books Against Nestorius; Against Diodore and Theodore; Scholia on The Incarnation*, Library of Fathers of the Church 47 (Oxford, 1881).

T. Randell, *Commentary on John* 2, Library of Fathers of the Church 48 (Oxford, 1885).

C.A. Heurtley, *On the Faith and The Creed. Dogmatic Teaching of the Church of the Fourth and Fifth Centuries* (incl. Cyril's dogmatic letters to Nestorius) (Oxford, 1886).

T.H. Bindley, *The Oecumenical Documents of the Faith* (dogmatic letters to Nestorius; Ep. 39 to John of Antioch) (1st ed. London, 1899; repr. 1906 & 1950).

J.B. Kidd, *Documents Illustrative of the History of the Church*, vol.2 (London 1938) (reproducing Heurtley for the dogmatic letters). The 3 letters and the Letter to John of Antioch turn up in several other florilegia volumes subsequently, e.g. E. R. Hardy, *The Christology of the Later Fathers* [London. 1954]).

A more imaginative and varied collection of Cyrilline translations is found in:

L.R. Wickham, *Cyril of Alexandria: Select Letters* (Oxford, 1983).

The complete Letters of Cyril (including some only extant in Coptic) have also been rendered by:

J.I. McEnerney, *St Cyril of Alexandria: Letters*, Fathers of the Church 76-77 (Washington 1987).

A full study of the theology and history of the Ephesine crisis, together with new translations of the key controversial texts from Cyril, and the synodical account of Nestorius' condemnation can be found in:

J.A. McGuckin, *St Cyril of Alexandria. The Christological Controversy* (Brill: Leiden, 1994).

B. Select Bibliography of General Studies

Bethune-Baker. J., *Introduction to the Early History of Christian Doctrine* (London, 1903).

Davis, L.D., *The First Seven Ecumenical Councils (325-787)* (Wilmington DE, 1987).

Frend, W.H.C., *The Rise of the Monophysite Movement* (Cambridge, 1979).

_____, *The Rise of Christianity* (Philadelphia, 1984).

Gregory, T.E., *Vox Populi. Popular Opinion and Violence in the Religious Controversies of the Fifth Century AD* (Columbus, 1979).

Hall, S.G., *Doctrine and Practice in the Early Church* (London, 1991) 211-222.

Holum, K.G., *Theodosian Empresses: Women and Imperial Dominion in Late Antiquity* (London, 1982).

Kelly, J.N.D., *Early Christian Doctrines*, 5th ed. (London-New York, 1978).

Meyendorff, J., *Christ in Eastern Christian Thought* (Washington, 1969).

Ottley, R.L., *The Doctrine of the Incarnation* vol. 2 (London. 1896).

Pelikan, J., *The Christian Tradition* vol.1. *The Emergence of the Catholic Tradition (100-600)* (Chicago-London, 1971).

Prestige, G.L., *God in Patristic Thought* (London, 1936).

_____, *Fathers and Heretics* (London, 1940).

Sellers, R.V., *Two Ancient Christologies: A study in the Christological Thought of the Schools of Alexandria and Antioch in the early History of Christian Doctrine* (London, 1940).

_____, *The Council of Chalcedon* (London, 1953).

Young, F., *From Nicaea to Chalcedon* (London, 1983).

Wolfson H.A., *The Philosophy of the Church Fathers*, vol.1 (Cambridge, MA 1956).

C. Select Bibliography of Cyrilline Studies

Berthold, G.C., "Cyril of Alexandria and the Filioque," *Stud Pat.* 19, 2 (Louvain 1989) 143-147.

Burghardt, W.J., *The Image of God in Man according to Cyril of Alexandria* (Washington, 1957).

_____, "St Cyril of Alexandria," *New Catholic Encyclopedia*, 4, 571-576 (New York, 1967).

von Campenhausen, H., *The Fathers of the Greek Church* (E.T.) (New York, 1959; London 1963), ch.12.

Chadwick, H., "Eucharist and Christology in the Nestorian Controversy," *JTS* (NS) 2 (1951) 145-164.

van den Dries, J., *The Formula of St Cyril of Alexandria: Mia Physis tou Theou Logou Sesarkomene* (Diss.) (Rome, 1939).

Gebremedhin, E., *Life-Giving Blessing. An Inquiry into the Eucharistic Doctrine of Cyril of Alexandria* (Uppsala, 1977).

Grillmeier, A., *Christ in Christian Tradition*, vol. 1 (2nd ed.) (London, 1975), 473-487.

Hardy, E.R., *Christian Egypt: Church and People* (New York, 1952).

_____, "The further education of Cyril of Alexandria, 412-444: Questions and Problems," *Stud Pat.* 17, 1 (1982) 116-122.

Kerrigan, A., "S. Cyril of Alexandria: Interpreter of the Old Testament," *Analecta Biblica* 2 (Rome, 1952).

_____, "The Objects of the Literal and Spiritual Senses of the New Testament according to St Cyril of Alexandria," *Stud Pat* 1 (TU 63) (Berlin, 1957), 354-374.

Koen, L., *The Saving Passion. Incarnational and Soteriological Thought in Cyril of Alexandria's Comm. on the Gospel According to St John* (Uppsala, 1991).

McCoy, J.D., "Philosophical Influences on the Doctrine of the Incarnation in Athanasius and Cyril of Alexandria," *Encounter* (Indianapolis) 38 (1977) 362-391.

McGuckin, J.A., "Christian Asceticism and the Early School of Alexandria," *Studies in Church History*, vol. 22 (Cambridge, 1985), pp. 25-39.

_____, *The Transfiguration of Christ in Scripture and Tradition* (New York, 1987).

_____, "The Concept of Orthodoxy in Ancient Christianity," *Patristic and Byzantine Review, 8, 1, (1989), 5-23.*

_____, "The Influence of the Isis Cult on St Cyril of Alexandria's Christology," *Studia Patristica* 24 (Leuven, 1992), 191-199.

_____, "Origen on the Jews," *Studies in Church History* 29 (Cambridge, 1992), 1-13.

_____, *St Cyril of Alexandria. The Christological Controversy* (Brill: Leiden, 1994).

Meijering, E.P., "Some reflections on Cyril of Alexandria's rejectiction of Anthropomorphism," in (ibid.) *God Being History* (Amsterdam, Oxford, 1975), 128-132.

_____, "Cyril of Alexandria on the Platonists and the Trinity," in (ibid.) *God Being History* (Amsterdam, Oxford, 1975), 114-127.

Nau, F., "St Cyril and Nestorius," *ROC* 15 (1910), 365-391; 16 (1911), 1-54.

Newman, J.H., "On St Cyril's formula: Mia Physis Sesarkomene," in *Tracts Theological and Ecclesiastical* (London, 1874), 283-336.

Norris, R.A., "Christological models in Cyril of Alexandria," *Stud Pat.* 13 (1975), 255-268.

Parvis, P.M., "The Commentary on Hebrews and the Contra Theodorum of Cyril of Alexandria," *JTS* (NS) 26 (1975), 415-419.

Payne-Smith, R., *Commentary on the Gospel of St Luke by St Cyril Patriarch of Alexandria* (2 vols. E.T.) (Oxford, 1859).

Romanides, J.S., "St Cyril's 'One physis or hypostasis of God the Logos incarnate' and Chalcedon," *GOTR* 10 (1964-65), 82-107.

Santer, M., "Ek Pneumatos Agiou kai Marias tes Parthenou," *JTS* 22 (1971), 162-171.

_____, "The authorship and occasion of Cyril of Alexandria's Sermon on the Virgin (*Hom. Diversae iv*)," *Stud. Pat.* 12 (1975), 144-150.

Siddals, R.M., "Oneness and Difference in the Christology of Cyril of Alexandria," *Stud Pat.* 18, 1 (Oxford, 1983), 207f.

_____, "Logic and Christology in Cyril of Alexandria," *JTS* (NS) 38 (1987), 341-367.

Souvay, C.L., "The Twelve Anathematizations of St Cyril," *CHR* 5 (1926), 627-635.

Tsirpanlis, C., "Christological aspects of the thought of St Cyril of Alexandria," chs. 1-3 in (ibid.) *Greek Patristic Theology* (New York, 1979).

Wickham, L.R., *Cyril of Alexandria: Select Letters* (E.T.) (Oxford, 1983).

_____, "Symbols of the Incarnation in Cyril of Alexandria," in *Typos, Symbol, Allegorie bei den östlichen Vatern und ihren Parallelen im Mittelalter*, edd. M Schmidt and C.F. Geyer (Regensburg, 1982), 41-53.

_____, "Cyril of Alexandria," *Encyclopedia of Early Christianity* (New York, 1990), 249-250.

Wiles, M.F., "The nature of the early debate about Christ's human soul," *JEH* 16 (1965), 139-151.

Wilken, R.L., "Tradition, Exegesis, and the Christological Controversies," *Church History* 34 (1965), 123-145.

_____, "Exegesis and the History of Theology: Some Reflections on the Adam-Christ typology in Cyril of Alexandria," *Church History* 35 (1966), 139-156.

_____, *Judaism and the Early Christian Mind: A study of Cyril of Alexandria's Exegesis and Theology* (London 1971).

Wolfson, H.A., "Philosophical implications of Arianism and Apollinarism," *DOP* 12 (1958), 3-28.

Young, F.M., "Christological ideas in the Greek Commentaries on the Epistle to the Hebrews," *JTS* (NS) 20 (1969), 150-163.

_____, "A re-consideration of Alexandrian Christology," *JEH* 22 (1971), 103-114.

_____, *From Nicaea to Chalcedon* (London, 1983), pp. 213-229, 240-265.

_____, "Exegetical Method and Scriptural Proof-The Bible in Doctrinal Debate," *Stud. Pat.* 19 (1989), 291-304.

D. Select Bibliography on Antiochene Christology

Abramowski, L., and Goodman A.E. (Edd.), *A Nestorian Collection of Christological Texts*, vol. 1 (Syriac); vol.2, Introduction, E.T., and Indices (Cambridge, 1972).

Anastos, M.V., "Nestorius was orthodox," DOP 16 (1962), 119-140.

Bethune-Baker, J.F., *Nestorius and His Teaching* (Cambridge, 1908).

Braaten, C.E., "Modern Interpretations of Nestorius," *Church History* 32 (1963), 251-267.

Chesnut, R.C., "The Two Prosopa in Nestorius' Bazaar of Heraclides," *JTS* (NS) 29 (1978), 392-408.

Dewart, J., *The Theology of Grace of Theodore of Mopsuestia* (Washington, 1971).

_____, "The notion of 'Person' underlying the Christology of Theodore Mopsuestia," *Stud Pat.* 12 (1975), 199-207.

Driver, G.R. and Hodgson, L., *The Bazaar of Heraclides* (Oxford, 1925).

Greer, R.A., *Theodore of Mopsuestia. Exegete and Theologian* (London, 1961).

_____, "The Image of God and the Prosopic Union in Nestorius'

Bazaar of Heraclides," in *Lux in Lumine*, (Ed.) R.A. Norris, Essays to Honour W.N. Pittenger (New York, 1966), 46-61.

_____, "The Antiochene Christology of Diodore of Tarsus," *JTS* 17 (1966), 327-341.

_____, *The Captain of Our Salvation* (Tübingen, 1973).

Hodgson, L., "The Metaphysic of Nestorius," *JTS* 19 (1918), 46-55.

Loofs, F., *Nestorius and his place in the History of Christian Doctrine* (Cambridge, 1914).

McGuckin, J.A., "The christology of Nestorius of Constantinople," *PBR* 7, 2-3 (1988), 93-129.

_____, "Did Augustine's Christology Depend on Theodore of Mopsuestia?" *Heythrop Journal* 31 (1990), 39-52.

McKenzie, J.L., "Annotations on the Christology of Theodore of Mopsuestia," *Theological Studies* 19 (1958), 345-373.

McNamara, J., "Theodore of Mopsuestia and the Nestorian Heresy," *ITQ* 19 (1952), 254-268; ibid. 20 (1953), 172-191.

_____, "Theodoret of Cyrus and the unity of Person in Christ," *ITQ* 22 (1955), 313- 328.

Norris, R.A., *Manhood and Christ. A Study of the Christology of Theodore of Mopsuestia* (Oxford, 1963).

Patterson, L., *Theodore Mopsuestia and Modern Thought* (London 1926).

Romanides, J.S., "Highlights in the Debate over Theodore of Mopsuestia's Christology and Some Suggestions for a Fresh Approach," *GOTR* 5 (1959-1960), 140-185.

Sellers, R.V., *Two Ancient Christologies* (London, 1940).

Sullivan, F.A., *The Christology of Theodore of Mopsuestia* (Rome, 1956).

Turner, H.E.W., "Nestorius reconsidered," *Stud. Pat.* 13 (1975), 306-321.

Vine, A.R., *An Approach to Christology: An interpretation and development of some elements in the metaphysic and christology of Nestorius as a way of approach to an orthodox christology compatible with modern thought* (London. 1948).

Wiles, M.F., "Theodore of Mopsuestia as Representative of the Antiochene School," *Cambridge History of the Bible*, vol.1 (1970), 489-510.

Young, F.M., *From Nicaea to Chalcedon* (London 1983), 182-240.

Index

A

Adam 57, 60, 62, 64, 105-106, 115, 126

Alexandria, city of 9-12, 31
Jewish community 9, 13-14

Alexandria, patriarchate of 9-10, 18, 23-24, 28, 31

Andrew of Samosata 46

Antidosis Idiomatum ("Communication of Idioms") 45
See also "Exchange of Properties"

apathos epathen 44
See also suffering

Apollinarist doctrine 40, 42, 46

"Appropriation Theory" 45
See also "Exchange of Properties"

Athanasius, Saint 9-11, 17, 31-32, 35

Atonement 35

Augusta Pulcheria, the 17, 21, 23

B

Beatific Vision 35

C

Celestine, pope 22-24, 26

"Christ" title 65-66, 87

Clement of Alexandria 10

"Communication of Idioms" 44
See also "Exchange of Properties"

Constantinople 11, 14, 16-17, 20-22, 24, 26-27
council of (381) 10, 23
council of (553) 15, 30-31
patrtriarchate of 10, 16, 28

Council of Constantinople (381) 10, 23

Council of Constantinople (553) 15, 30-31

Council of Ephesus (431) 15, 20, 25-29

cross, the 118, 121, 125, 129, 133
Christ's death on 56, 70, 85, 112, 121-122

Cyril of Alexandria 24-25, 29-30
administration 12, 14-15
christological doctrine 32-38, 40-41, 44, 46
death 31
early life 11-12
and Nestorius 19-24
theological method 36
theology 20
works 15-16, 30

D

death 43-45, 51, 55, 57-61, 68-70, 74, 101, 105-106, 112-116, 118, 120, 125-128, 130
fear of 58, 104-105, 114

deification 16, 35

Didymus the Blind 11

Diodore of Tarsus 17, 21, 29-30, 47

E

Emmanuel   52-53, 76, 78, 98
"Exchange of Properties"   44
    Appropriation Theory   45

F

Formula of Reunion   28-29

G

grace   33, 35, 43, 62-64, 76, 80-
    82, 88, 94-95, 97-98, 109, 117,
    119-120, 131
Gregory the Theologian, Saint
    10-11

H

Henosis   34, 40
    See also union
Holy Spirit   62, 65-67, 95-96, 98-
    100, 127
Hypatia   13

I

incarnation   16, 20, 33-38, 40-45,
    47, 51, 56-57, 59, 66, 79, 89,
    97, 112, 125, 132
Irenaeus, Saint   35

J

John Cassian, Saint   22
John Chrysostom, Saint   10-11
John of Antioch, archbishop   16,
    24-26, 28-29, 31
John the Baptist, Saint   100
John the Evangelist, Saint   53, 61,
    67, 69, 77, 81, 98, 120, 123-
    124, 131

M

marriage   62
Maximian, archbishop   28
Memnon, bishop   24-28
Menouthis Temple   12
monasticism   9
Moses   52-53, 70, 72, 78-79, 97,
    106, 116, 128
Mother of God   18-19, 25, 32, 45,
    52, 55, 64-65
    See also Theotokos

N

Nestorius, archbishop   17-23, 26-
    31, 33, 36, 43, 45-47, 52
    administration   16-17
    and Council of Ephesus   24-25
    and Cyril of Alexandria   19-23
    and the Roman Church   22-23
    theology of   18-19, 33-34

O

Orestes, governor   13, 14
Origen   10, 31

P

pagans, paganism 12, 35, 47, 49-50
    in Alexandria   9-10, 12-14
Pantaenus   10
Patriarchate of Alexandria   9-10,
    18, 23, 28, 31
Patriarchate of Constantinople
    10, 16, 28
Paul, Saint 49, 54-55, 58, 61-63, 66,
    69-70, 73, 78, 80, 82, 84-86, 89-90,
    92-93, 95-97, 99, 106, 108, 110-
    112, 114, 116, 118, 121, 127-129

Pelagianism   22
Peter, Saint   94, 101-102, 104, 117, 126
prayer   102-103, 125
Proclus, archbishop   18, 22, 30
prophets   34, 41, 65, 72, 97-98
prosopon   83, 109
"psychic consciousness"   41

R

resurrection   37, 59, 62, 115, 118, 126
Roman Church   24
   and Nestorius   22
Roman Empire   9

S

salvation   43, 58-60, 68, 89, 112-113, 116, 118, 132
Shenoudi of Atripe, Saint   15
sin   55-61, 64, 69, 89-90, 93-94, 105-107, 109, 113, 115
Sisinnius, archbishop   16, 21
Son of David   80, 82-83, 85, 93
Son of Man   87, 93-94, 104, 118, 131-132
soul, the   55, 57, 64, 67
   and the body   38, 40, 64, 78

suffering
   of Christ   43-44, 104, 110, 112-118, 121, 125-127, 129-131, 133
   human   43, 102, 104
Synod of Ephesus (449)   31
Synod of the Oak (403)   10-11

T

Theodore of Mopsuestia   17-18, 21, 29-30, 47
Theodoret of Cyr   16, 31, 46
Theodosius, emperor   13, 21, 26-27
Theophilus, Saint   10-12, 31
theosis   34-35
Theotokos   18, 45
   See also Mother of God
Trinity, the   73, 96, 127
"Two Sons"   18, 30, 39-40

U

union
   of body and soul   38
   of God and Man   35, 37-38
   "hypostatic union"   40
   term   34, 40, 73-74
   See also Henosis

W

Wickham, L.   14

Index of Biblical References

OLD TESTAMENT

Genesis

19:26	53

Exodus

4:3	53
16:	72

Numbers

16:11	72

Deuteronomy

8:3	49
10:22	78
17:13	97

Joshua

3:7	53

1 Samuel

8:5	72
8:7	72

1 Kings

19:10	51

Psalms

21:11	79
22:7	107
22:18	107
40:6-8 LXX	121
44:7-8	66
45:6-7	67
50:3 LXX	111
63:8	73
81:9	86
81:10 LXX	73
90:1	54
94:22	54
104:15	49
105:15	65
136:12	52

Proverbs

9:18 LXX	51
26:11	50

Isaiah

7:14	52
24:13-14	101
42:8	76
44:20	50
53:9	90
60:1-2	101
63:9	116
63:9 LXX	110, 132

Jeremiah

Jer 8:23	76
23:6	112

Joel

1:5	96
2:28	78

Amos

7:14-15	74

Habakkuk		26:38	104
1:5	61	26:39	104, 126
2:6 LXX	50	27:26	103
3:13	65	27:40	129
		27:46	102, 105
Zephaniah		28:19	127
2:1-2 LXX	74	*Mark*	
		10:27	79
NEW TESTAMENT		10:34	104
Matthew		*Luke*	
1:21	87	1:15	98
1:23	52	1:30-31	87
4:2	107	1:76	109
4:4	49	2:52	109
4:10	124		
8:24	107	*John*	
10:28	103	1:1	58, 123
12:33	125	1:5	90
13:41	94	1:11-12	81
13:55	111	1:12	63
14:33	94	1:13	62
16:7	94	1:14	53, 56, 67, 69, 77
16:14	111	1:16	67, 91, 100
16:16-17	94	1:18	121
16:22	104	1:29-30	109
16:23	104	1:29-31	94
16:24	103	1:32-34	99
17:26	75	2:19	119
18:11	127	3:12	93
19:4	62	3:13	93
21:38	81	3:16	120
22:29	79	3:31	61, 98, 124
22:42	82	4:6	107
22:43-45	82	4:22	116
23:9	63	5:21	119
25:40	72	6:38-39	124
26:37	104	6:42	111

6:51	132	9:5	84, 116
6:51, 33	131	10:6-9	71
6:53	131	10:8	57
8:40	107	15:15-16	108
8:58	93		
10:3	107	*1 Corinthians*	
10:11, 18	127	1:13	93
10:30	125	1:18, 24	118
10:33	91	1:22-25	129
10:37-38	95	1:23	99
10:38	95	2:8	116
13:31-32	118	3:10-11	133
14:6	90, 129	3:16	96
14:9	107, 125	4:7	90-91
14:23	96	5:7	128
17:5	86, 123	6:17	73
20:17	63	6:19, 20	128
20:22-23	100	6:20	111
		8:5-6	87
Acts		8:6	95
2:24	126	15:10	90
3:22	97	15:17	57
10:38	95	15:20	126
13:41	61	15:22	106, 115
20:30	50	15:45	57, 105, 126
		15:47-49	64
Romans		15:49	61
1:16	118	15:47	124
1:21-23	50		
1:22	90	*2 Corinthians*	
1:28	76	1:19	90
5:14	106	4:6	108
5:15	106	4:16	78
6:3	127	5:15	128
6:5	59, 115	5:17	88, 105, 114
8:3	60	5:21	56, 69, 115
8:3-4	89	10:5	99
8:15	80	13:3-4	119
8:32	69, 114		

Galatians

1:1	110
1:11-12	110
2:19-20	128
3:13	56
3:24	70
4:4	60
4:4-5	68
6:14	112

Ephesians

1:10	132
1:19-21	119
1:20-21	119
1:21	68, 82
3:14-17	80
4:5	109, 127
5:1-2	111

Philippians

2:5-8	54
2:5-9	85
2:5-11	122
2:6	108
2:6f	58
2:7	55, 75, 119
2:8	55, 70
2:10-11	133

Colossians

1:15	108
1:15-18	116
1:18	63, 126
1:21-22	128

1 Timothy

3:16	132

Titus

2:11-13	90

Hebrews

1:3	54, 86
1:5	82
1:13	82
2:9, 10-17	114
2:10	112
2:11	99
2:11-12	66
2:14	89
2:14-17	58
2:17	64, 97, 107
3:1	97
4:15	58
5:7	104
5:7-9	102
9:23	113
9:23-26	113
10:14	114
10:19-20	111
10:28-29	117
12:2	55, 70, 116, 129
13:4	62
13:8	92
13:12	128

James

2:1	101

1 Peter

1:18-19	111
2:20-21	103
2:22	105
3:18	117
4:1	129
4:14	101

2 Peter		*1 John*	
2:1	76	1:7	60
2:21-22	50	1 2:19	50
		1 4:2-3	88
		1 4:14-15	88
		1 5:20	131